THE CAREER RESOURCE LIBRARY

Careers
in
Modeling

Kerri O'Donnell

The Rosen Publishing Group, Inc.
NEW YORK

My thanks to Ken, Catherine, and Erin for their support

Published in 2001 by The Rosen Publishing Group, Inc.
29 East 21st Street, New York, NY 10010

Cover photo by Ira Fox

Library of Congress Cataloging in Publication Data

O'Donnell, Kerri, 1972–
Careers in modeling / Kerri O'Donnell.—1st ed.
p. cm. — (The career resource library)
Includes bibliographical references and index.
ISBN 0-8239-3183-8 (library binding)
1. Models (Persons)—Vocational guidance—Juvenile literature. [1. Models (Persons)—Vocational guidance. 2. Fashion—Vocational guidance. 3. Vocational guidance.] I. Title. II. Series.
HD8039.M77 O36 2001

2001001192

Manufactured in the United States of America

Contents

Introduction

The word "modeling" conjures up a variety of vivid images, ranging from photos of thin women with pouty lips sauntering down a Calvin Klein catwalk, or a magazine spread of fresh-faced teenagers modeling the latest clothes and hottest hairstyles in *Seventeen* magazine, to the voluptuous women wearing next to nothing in the *Sports Illustrated* swimsuit issue, or the glowing face of Isabella Rosellini or Elizabeth Hurley promoting a multitude of beauty products.

A Model Image

Maybe you read all the fashion magazines and think that nothing would be cooler than gracing those glossy pages and having millions of people admire you. Maybe you think of those chiseled, lean, handsome guys that sport Armani suits, or of those rugged, outdoorsy types in the J. Crew catalog. What would it be like, you think, to be sought after for the mere fact that you have the look of the moment?

Modeling Equals Beauty?

The concept of beauty is the foundation of the modeling industry—or more specifically, that most people want to look at, be surrounded by, and be viewed as an ideal that is aesthetically pleasing. However, beauty is subjective. Ask 100 people to describe their concept of beauty, and you'll very likely get 100 totally different answers. Ideas about what is beautiful can vary from country to country—what is considered beautiful in France or Italy is different than what is considered beautiful in Zimbabwe or Afghanistan.

The Fickle World of Fashion

A career in modeling requires one basic thing—that you be physically attractive. However, a man or woman need not be conventionally beautiful to make the grade in the modeling industry. The world of fashion is famously fickle. With the rapidity at which trends change, the look that's hot this month could be ice cold next month, or even next week. Today, there is a very strong market for models with distinctive features and exotic looks that will catch the public's eye in a new way. In order to stay one step ahead of the "look of the moment," the industry must constantly reinvent itself. As a result, models from all different ethnic backgrounds are embraced and sought after much more so than they were even ten years ago.

Young women and men with modeling fever no longer have to fit into such a stereotypical mold to succeed in the business. Female models need not have flowing blonde locks, limpid blue eyes, and alabaster skin, and male models don't have to be cookie-cutter handsome.

In a recent article appearing in *Vogue* magazine, famous fashion designer Helmut Lang summed it up effectively: "What we're trying to avoid is plain, common beauty . . . individual character is more important." In other words, an interesting look can indeed get you noticed. That's what the business of modeling is all about—catching the public's eye and making enough of an impression to keep their attention. If you think you're model material, it's important to market yourself with confidence.

Beauty for Sale

A career in modeling is, for the most part, a career in which you sell your image along with a product in order to enhance that product's appeal. It follows a sort of code where people want to recreate for themselves a look or style that appeals to their idea of beauty.

By buying the clothing, jewelry, makeup, or handbags that a model sports in an ad, the consumer is trying to become more like the image that the model represents. This is not a new concept. Hundreds of years ago, the lower classes looked to nobility to show them what was acceptable, thinking that they could raise their social status if they emulated the fashions of the rich and powerful.

A Tough Business

Modeling is an extremely competitive industry. Because it places such a strong emphasis on youth, most models' careers are short when compared to the careers of people working in more "traditional" jobs. In the modeling industry, youth equals beauty, with a few exceptions. This is especially true for female models, who on average have careers that last just a few years. In recent years, however, there has been an attempt to feature "older" models in ad campaigns.

Compared to ten years ago, today there are more older models finding steady work modeling clothes in catalogs and representing cosmetic lines. Companies want to win over the largest possible buying audience to ensure themselves the greatest profit, and they have realized that they can do this most effectively by not alienating any particular consumer group.

However, the truth of the matter is that the number of aspiring models who don't "make it" greatly outnumber the ones who do. Despite the fact that the industry as a whole has opened up to different ideas of what beauty is, it's important to realize that modeling may be one of the most daunting careers that there is. Models (and aspiring models) are judged first and foremost by their looks, not on their knowledge or beliefs, and this can be tough to accept.

If you think that you've got what it takes—if you have attractive hands or feet or especially lustrous hair and would like to find out about being a parts model, or if you think you'd be a good plus-size or petite model, or if you think you'd be good on the catwalk—you'll need to know what to do next.

Making it in the modeling business takes steadfastness, knowledge, talent, and above all, perseverance. The upcoming chapters will give you the facts and tips you need to be as well prepared as you can be.

Modeling: The Big Picture

1

One of the most common assumptions about modeling is that it is the most glamorous and exciting job you could have. It's a good idea to burst this balloon from the outset—this is absolutely false. Though this level of fame and success does occur, it is achieved by a tiny percentage of those in the business. However, when most of us think of modeling, we think of the images of models that pack the biggest wallop—the models who grace the glossy pages of the biggest fashion magazines wearing $20,000 outfits. In the early to mid-1990s, there were the "supermodels"— Cindy Crawford, Naomi Campbell, Christy Turlington, and Linda Evangelista—women who reigned over the fashion industry and whose faces were everywhere you looked. While the era of the supermodel is over, there is a new batch of models whose names are synonymous with high fashion—models like Gisele Bundchen, Amber Valetta, Alex Wek, and Carmen Kass (who won VH1's Model of the Year Award in 2000). However, as with the supermodels, for every one of these women, there are thousands of models who are completely unknown.

Just the Facts

While modeling may seem like the coolest, most glamorous career ever, it is in fact hard, demanding work. Models spend hour upon hour under hot lights. They have to contend with unscrupulous agents, rigorous schedules, and tough competition. Modeling can at times be a daunting career, but understanding how the modeling industry operates and knowing your role within it can make all the difference.

Realistic Goals

It is great to dream big—if you always settled for what comes easily, life would be lackluster at best. So aim high, but keep in mind that going into modeling does not mean that you will achieve great stardom or make millions of dollars a year. You can make good (and even great) money as a model, but it is important to keep things in perspective.

Earning Potential

On average, the bigger modeling agencies in New York City (the modeling center of the world) and Paris (the fashion center of the world) expect their newer models to make approximately $40,000 during their first year of representation—if not, the models may not be kept on an agency's roster. This is considered a realistic expectation of a starting model, not the millions of dollars that come to mind when we think of those famous models' faces we see all over the place. Of course, $40,000 is a tidy sum for a teenager, but many hopeful models become disenchanted when they don't earn the kind of money they associate with the big models. Knowing the facts can help you avoid setting yourself up for any disappointment later on.

A model with a solid career who is signed with a well-established agency can make $50,000 a year or more, depending on the market in which he or she works. The average annual salary for a successful model in New York City is between $80,000 and $150,000, and the top models make upwards of $200,000. Supermodels—those most rare of models— can make anywhere from half a million dollars per year to several million, but again, this is unusual and applies to a tiny percentage of all models. The top male models can bring in between $100,000 and $1 million, and their careers can typically last much longer than that of female models.

Having a Master Plan

While a model in a smaller city can easily make over $100 an hour, the work may be sporadic, and it can take a little while to gain the exposure needed to get more jobs. For that reason, it is important that you have other skills to fall back on to support yourself. Many models become commercial actors or spokespeople after they stop modeling, since both of these options require many of the same skills as modeling—namely that you know how to promote a product. Of course, there is no limit to what you can do in the future, but it's wise to have a viable game plan.

Because modeling focuses so strongly on youth, this is probably not a career that will last for a long time. By developing other skills, talents, and interests, you'll ensure that you are well-prepared for life after modeling. Getting a well-rounded education is very important. Consider Christy Turlington, who began modeling as a teenager. After making millions of dollars as a supermodel, she recently enrolled at New York University to work toward a B.A. She realized that there's a whole world out there, and modeling is just a tiny slice of it.

Assessing Your Potential

Maybe you've wanted to be a model since you were ten years old, or maybe people have suggested that you model and you've just recently decided to pursue it as a career. Whatever the case may be, the first step in determining if modeling is for you is assessing your modeling potential. This can be quite a task. After all, it is difficult for us to look at ourselves objectively and take account of our shortcomings, but doing so now may save you from unnecessary letdowns later.

Do You Have What It Takes?

- First and foremost, a model must be ambitious. It can't be overstated: Modeling is a tough business to break into. There are thousands and thousands of hopeful models out there and the competition is fierce. If you are going to make it as a model, you have to be prepared to work hard. Agents will not come to you. The work will not come to you.

- Confidence is also absolutely necessary. If you are self-assured, you can sell anything, and clients can sense this immediately. The road to modeling success is riddled with rejections based on issues that usually have little to do with you. Rejection is a way of life in the modeling industry, and this can be very difficult to deal with if you don't have a good amount of confidence in yourself.

- A model must be intelligent and must have a good business sense to communicate effectively with agents, clients, photographers, and so on. This degree of professionalism is a must.

- The ability to be independent is also important. Modeling by its very nature can be an isolating experience—a model is on the go constantly and may have to travel alone for a particular assignment. If you don't like being alone, this could be difficult.

- A model must be well organized. As you get more and more jobs, there will be all kinds of names, dates, and places to keep straight. Models must get to their appointments promptly or they may risk losing out on jobs.

- It is also important for a model to be disciplined. Because so much relies on a model's looks, a healthy diet, exercise routine, and adequate sleep schedule must be maintained. You must have the willpower to avoid any practices or substances that could affect your looks or ability to perform a job responsibly.

• Physical attributes are a key factor. Although some specialized modeling fields, such as the plus-size and petite markets, have a need for models of different shapes and sizes—and some commercial advertising may call for "average-looking" models to sell a particular product—typically, a model must be tall, thin, and attractive.

If you feel that both your physical and personality traits fit the bill, it's time to figure out how you can get your career started.

Types of Modeling

2

A career in modeling has limitless possibilities. Because there are so many avenues your career can take, giving you a breakdown of the different branches in the industry will help you have a better sense of what your options are.

Editorial Print Models

Editorial print models are the models we see in fashion magazines where their images are being used to sell clothing, makeup, jewelry, etc. "Editorial print" refers to the photos in magazines, including the almighty cover shot. If a model scores just one magazine cover shot, it can be like knocking down the first domino—he or she is then much more likely to be booked for major fashion ad campaigns and may even be chosen to appear on a runway to model clothing for the industry's hottest designers. This exposure can lead to where the real money lies: contract work for cosmetics, fragrances, or designer clothing. And the more editorial print assignments you have under your belt, the more expansive your portfolio, or "book," will be. Putting together a portfolio will be discussed further in chapter 6, but in a nutshell, a portfolio is how a model sells himself or herself to a prospective client. It is a comprehensive collection of photographs that shows the model's versatility.

Sonya's Big Break

Sonya had wanted to be a model since she was twelve years old. Her parents agreed that when she turned sixteen, she could contact some modeling agencies. A few weeks after she turned sixteen, Sonya—with a lot of hard work and patience—found an agency to represent her.

Sonya and her parents lived in a midsized city, and most of the work Sonya got consisted of clothing shoots for catalogs and an occasional ad in a local magazine. Sonya's portfolio grew, and soon her agency recommended that she meet with a few of their contacts in New York. It was an exciting proposition, but Sonya was a bit apprehensive. New York was a tough market. Sonya's parents told her to view it as a learning experience and to do her best.

The meetings in New York went well, and Sonya was asked to pose for some shots that would possibly be used for a magazine cover. The next thing she knew, her face was on the cover of a teen fashion magazine. The exposure from the cover shoot was tremendous.

Offers began pouring in, and Sonya found herself in the running for a major designer-clothing campaign, which she soon snagged. One magazine cover had made the industry sit up and take notice, and she eventually found herself with more success than she had ever dreamed of.

Earning Potential

Editorial print work is highly coveted because of the exposure it can provide, and as a result the pay is modest. Most models can figure on a range of about $100 to $400 a day for many long hours of demanding work. This applies for magazine cover-shot photo sessions, too. Another positive aspect of editorial print jobs is that they can give you great tear sheets for your portfolio. "Tear sheet" is modeling lingo for a photograph taken of a model that appears in a magazine. The model can add that tear sheet to his or her portfolio. The more tear sheets a model has, the more marketable his or her portfolio is to prospective modeling agencies that could then send the model out on more high-profile jobs.

Physical Requirements

Editorial models—or print models, as they are often called—usually need to meet some standardized physical requirements. Female models should be at least five feet, nine inches, tall and about a size six. They typically have a 34B cup size, a waistline that averages between twenty-three and twenty-four inches, and hips that average between thirty-four and thirty-five inches around at the widest point. The average weight is about 120 pounds, and models' bodies are expected to be well toned.

Male models should be no shorter than five feet, eleven inches tall, and usually no taller than about six feet, two inches. In a shoot with shorter female models, a male model who is taller than this may throw off the symmetry of a photo. Male models are generally expected to wear a jacket size of forty or forty-two regular and have a chest measurement of about thirty-eight to forty inches. The standard waistline measurement is between thirty-two and thirty-four inches, and male models are expected to have an inseam that also measures about thirty-two to thirty-four inches. This measurement is taken along the inside seam of a pair of pants, from the crotch to the bottom of the ankle. The average weight of a male model is about 165 pounds.

Because advertisers are always looking for a unique style to sell their product, male models with thinner, more wiry frames can often find a lot of work. Designers of men's clothing have been moving in this direction, and their ad campaigns often feature tall, lanky men who are more slight of build than the typical male model. A man who is shorter or taller than the industry standard may find success in commercial print modeling (see below) or television.

That Special Something

Success in editorial modeling relies on much more than having an attractive face, a nice body, and a great smile. It helps for a model to have a comfortable way with the camera. It may sound trite, but a model who instinctually knows how to convey a particular emotion with a single glance (and can do so convincingly and seemingly without effort) can virtually guarantee himself or herself more work in the future. The model's job, quite simply, is to understand the photographer's artistic vision and carry out the photographer's direction.

A model who has a keen sense of fashion and style and is able to improvise will be better equipped to creatively fulfill a photographer's demands. For instance, if a photographer wants a shoot to have a 1920s feel to it, but the model does not know anything about the style of that era, the photographs will likely not have the impact they could. The bottom line: Models need to be knowledgeable, creative, and imaginative.

High-Fashion Models

High-fashion models—a term that applies mostly to female models—are essentially glorified editorial models. These are the models whose faces you see so often that you feel like you know them personally. These models work in the world of high fashion, or haute couture, where they model the clothes of the industry's leading designers. High-fashion models are photographed wearing the collections of designers such as Versace, Armani, Calvin Klein, Prada, Chanel, and Valentino. These photographs are seen primarily in high-profile fashion magazines with worldwide distribution, such as *Vogue*, *Harper's Bazaar*, *W*, and *Elle*. They also frequently appear in designers' runway shows.

Earning Potential

High-fashion models typically make more money than any other type of model. Successful high-fashion models can make thousands of dollars for a good day's work. Some high-fashion models—the "girls of the moment"—may make $10,000 a day, and some make even more than that. While not all high-fashion models make this much in a given day, they are compensated well for their time, usually making at least a few thousand dollars per day.

Physical Requirements

High-fashion models are usually between five feet, nine inches and six feet tall. In this area of modeling, height is especially important because the designer's clothes must fit the model's body just so. In the world of high fashion, a long, slender body is the fashion designer's ideal, as this body type is thought to best showcase the beauty and elegance of the clothing's cut.

For this reason, these models are exceptionally thin, usually between a size four and six. They generally have a bust size that measures between thirty-two and thirty-five inches (the average bra size is a 34B), a waistline that measures between twenty-two and twenty-five inches, and hips that average about thirty-four to thirty-five inches around the fullest part of the buttocks. Their average weight is about 120 pounds (and often less). Very few women are built this way, and the high-fashion industry is often criticized for the unhealthy idealization of this exceptionally thin body type.

The Realistic View

While high-fashion modeling is obviously one of the more "glamorous" types of modeling, and is therefore very alluring to models who are just starting out—it is important to keep in mind that a very small percentage of models actually become high-fashion models. While hard work and determination definitely play a large part in achieving success in this area, unfortunately it is often a matter of being in the right place at the right time—of catching the eye of a certain agent or photographer. If you wait for this to happen, you could be wasting a lot of valuable time that you could be using to search out good jobs that will give you more exposure and will help you add to your portfolio.

Runway Models

In years past, there was a definite distinction between runway models and editorial models. This is not so today. Instead, many editorial models stroll the catwalk for the ready-to-wear and haute couture fashion shows. For runway work, female models must be at least five feet, nine inches tall, although it is preferred that they be even taller. The rest of the physical requirements are the same as those listed for high fashion and editorial print models. Male models must be about six feet tall.

When it comes to gaining exposure, runway modeling can be enormously effective. Models must present themselves in a graceful and self-confident way. They must look as if the garments they are wearing were made just for them. An editorial model who does a successful print campaign for a designer will likely be asked to take a turn down that designer's runway when the designer shows his or her collection. The glamour factor can't be ignored—a good turn down the catwalk at a designer's show can turn around an unknown model's career in the blink of an eye.

Commercial Print Models

While editorial print models sell designer clothes, commercial print models sell everything else under the sun. We see commercial models on billboards and on the sides of buses, they smile at us from the pages of newspapers and magazines, they appear on travel brochures and posters, their smiling faces are on cereal boxes and containers of hair dye, and they appear in countless television commercials. Commercial modeling can be classified as either fashion advertising or product advertising. When you think of it, these models are salespeople who sell us products without uttering a single word—hence, they must be pretty good at what they do.

Earning Potential

In commercial modeling, the pay scale can vary widely, with fees ranging from $50 to $250 an hour. The amount a model is paid often depends on the type of job assigned and the city in which the assignment takes place. The pay for this kind of modeling is unpredictable—generally, an assignment that involves promoting a nationally distributed product will bring in more money than will a billboard ad for a local restaurant, for example. Financial remuneration depends on the budget of the client whose product or service is being advertised.

It is possible for a commercial model to earn $50,000 or more for a single job, if that job were to promote a successful product for a high-profile client. On the other hand, if the product being advertised has a limited demographic scope, it is possible for a commercial model to make much less money. Smaller clients pay less money, and for this reason it's important to do your research. If you know the kind of commercial work you'd like to do, be sure to have photos in your portfolio that will appeal to the clients you're targeting.

Physical Requirements

In commercial modeling, the physical requirements are not as rigid because the client is often looking for someone who will be seen as a "real" person who can connect with the public at large. The average height of a commercial model is five feet, eight inches, but this is not nearly as strict as it is in high-fashion or editorial print modeling. Models of all sizes and shapes can find work. Age is also not a factor, as many products benefit from either a more youthful or a more mature advertising approach.

Catalog Models

Catalog modeling is one of the main sources of income for most models. Companies hire models to help sell their clothing (or other products) via mail-order catalogs or brochures. J. Crew, Victoria's Secret, Land's End, and L.L. Bean are all examples of companies that use catalogs as their primary source of advertising. The model's job is to make the clothing (or products) look appealing, which in turn ups sales and increases revenue for the company. Catalog bookings can last anywhere from a few hours—to photograph an item or two—to a week or more on location to shoot an array of items.

The pay scale for catalog modeling varies, but a good catalog model can earn an impressive annual salary. A model can make about $150 an hour, and can make between $1,200 and $2,500 a day. Because photo shoots for catalogs involve taking many more shots per day than are taken for an editorial shoot, the most successful catalog models are those who can get the job done quickly, easily, and above all, professionally.

Specialty Modeling

If it seems as though there is no room in the modeling industry for models who don't meet the often stringent physical code for editorial models, take heart—there is, in fact, a world of opportunity open to those models who don't match the standard height requirements, don't wear a size six dress, or don't have exceptionally lovely hands or feet. These are all different kinds of specialty modeling, and these can be successful careers.

Plus-Size Modeling

The world of plus-size modeling is mostly geared toward female models. Plus-size modeling has undergone a remarkable surge in the past few years, mainly because the standard size of the average woman has steadily increased. It is estimated, for instance, that the average woman in the United States is between a size twelve and a size fourteen. For this reason, there is an increased demand for plus-size models to help sell the clothing that average women buy. Many of New York's big modeling agencies—such as Ford and Wilhelmina—have started plus-size divisions. Women's fashion magazines have also gotten in on the act. One magazine, *Mode*, features only plus-size women. Top fashion magazines, devoted exclusively to "straight-size" models, have begun to include spreads featuring larger models.

Earning Potential

The pay scale for plus-size modeling is comparable to that of straight-size modeling. Models can make about $1,200 to $1,500 a day for catalog work, and many make six-figure annual salaries. Generally, plus-size models can continue their careers for a longer period of time—sometimes well into their forties or fifties—because the market calls for older models to appeal to a large portion of the public's older, plus-size women.

Physical Requirements

Plus-size models are also often called "10/20" models because they can range in size from a ten to a twenty. Usually, models who get the most jobs wear a size twelve or fourteen. These models must meet many of the same standards as straight-size models. Their legs should be long, their necks should be long and graceful, and they must have a natural way with the camera. On average, most 10/20 models are between five feet, eight and five feet, eleven inches tall, their bust size measures between thirty-six and forty-two inches, their waistlines measure between twenty-six and thirty-two inches, and their hips measure between thirty-six and forty-five inches. They typically weigh between 140 and 170 pounds.

Petite Models

Up until a few years ago, there were agencies that solely represented petite models. According to these agencies' standards, petite models were between five feet, two inches and five feet, seven inches tall. The models who got the most work were usually at the taller end of this range, and this was despite the fact that petite clothing sizes are made for women a few inches shorter than this. Their proportions were comparable to straight-size models, but their bust, waist, and hip measurements were on average one to two inches smaller.

In recent years, petite models have been absorbed into agencies that primarily represent straight-size models. They are paid according to the same scale. An attractive model that is smaller in stature can indeed become a successful "beauty model," which means that his or her face is the focus of most of the photographs taken. The petite model has many avenues to pursue, ranging from cosmetic ads and product endorsements to television commercials and magazine covers. For these models, there is also the possibility of modeling for fashion designers' petite lines of clothing.

Physical Requirements

These models don't have to be a minimum of five feet, nine inches to get work. However, most petite models are between five feet, six inches and five feet, eight inches tall. It's important to note that a magazine cover shot or a cosmetics endorsement does not focus on the model's stature, but rather on her features—on what she "looks like."

If an agency or someone in the business tells you that you are too short to model, be sure to get another opinion. There are too many opportunities to let a few inches stand in your way of becoming a successful model.

Body-Parts Models

You've probably seen body-parts models all over the place and haven't even been aware of it. You may have seen them in advertisements in magazines or on television commercials, or even on magazine covers. Believe it or not, you often see body-parts models' beautiful feet, hands, and even washboard abs morphed onto the bodies of celebrities that appear on the covers of magazines and in product advertisements. Though these models get none of the glory, they are chosen to do such jobs based on the fact that they have body parts that photograph beautifully.

Physical Requirements

The requirements for body-parts models depend on the specific body part being modeled.

Hand Models

- Female models usually have a 6 1/2 to 7 1/2 glove size and wear a 4 1/2 to 5 1/2 ring.

- Male hand models usually have an 8 1/2 to 10 1/2 glove size, and are identified by the shape of their hands.

- The skin of the hands should be perfect, without any noticeable veins or scars.

- Models with long, thin fingers are usually chosen to advertise jewelry, while models with more square, strong-looking hands are used to advertise household items, like tools.

Foot and Leg Models

- These models can find work in editorial print, commercial print, and television commercials.

- Ads for women's shoes, feminine hygiene, and hosiery require models with long and shapely legs, slim ankles, and feet that are narrow, well shaped, and well pedicured.

- The average shoe size of a female foot model is a size six.

What is the downside of parts modeling? Maintaining perfection in the chosen body part or parts can become pretty demanding. Hand and feet models, for instance, must give themselves daily manicures and pedicures. They must avoid exposure to the sun, housework, and cooking for fear of irritation of the skin from harsh chemicals or burns from a hot stove. Many hand and feet models wear gloves all year long to protect their skin from the elements. And the smallest paper cut or scratch can wreak havoc on a model's work schedule!

Mark and His Manicure

When Mark says he makes a living with his hands, he means it. No, he doesn't build homes or fix cars. Mark is a hand model.

Mark has hands that look as if they were sculpted by Michelangelo himself. They are, in a word, perfect—and he gets paid well to have them photographed. His hands have been photographed to advertise rings and watches. They have been captured forever on film slathering on hand cream and carrying briefcases. Advertisers know that good hands help sell products.

Many of Mark's friends envy his job and kid him about how easy it is. But being a hand model means that Mark has to make certain sacrifices—he has to avoid doing things that most people would never even think twice about doing, like staining a new cabinet for his kitchen, handling sheets of paper (because of potential paper cuts), or even cooking dinner over a hot stove. If he were to stain, cut, or burn his hands—even a little—he could be out of work for days or even weeks until his hands heal completely.

Mark must also spend a good deal of time caring for his "perfect" hands. He must make sure they are always manicured and well moisturized. He even sleeps with gloves on . . . after applying cuticle oil and hand cream, of course. Being a hand model requires a lot of planning and strict regimens. If Mark's hands aren't in tip-top shape, potential clients will find another pair of hands to sell their products.

Contacting the Agencies

3

Once you've decided that you want to be a model—and you know a bit about the different kinds of modeling that exist—what do you do next? Although there are some models who choose to represent themselves and book their own jobs, this can be a tough way to go about things and can limit your opportunities since you have to make all of your contacts yourself. The standard procedure is to find an agency that will have an established list of clients and contacts and that can use its name to get your foot in the door.

What an Agent Does

A modeling agent—also called a booker—is essentially the link between the model and the modeling industry. An agent acts as the go-between and is responsible for setting up clients with models. An agent's job, quite simply, is to find you work. It is also the agent's responsibility to assess your strengths as a model, decide which kind of work you are best suited to—depending on your style and personality—and to devise a plan to ensure that you get plenty of good jobs, be they in editorial work, commercial work, etc. A good agent will have a strong sense of what area of the business would be the most beneficial for you. Then, your agent will go to work getting you jobs that you can add to your portfolio and sending you on "go-sees." Go-sees are appointments during which you "go and see" a prospective client.

An agent is responsible for promoting you. He or she will see to it that your face (or hands and feet, as the case may be) gets seen by those within the industry who can further your career, whether they are casting agents, fashion magazine editors, art directors, fashion designers, or photographers. These are the people who select models for jobs. An agent will guide you in putting together a great portfolio that will help market you to clients who may choose you to represent their product, whether that product is mascara or contact lenses, hand cream or ice cream, sneakers or stilettos.

A good agent who is well connected within the industry can be your lifeline in the often-turbulent waters of the modeling industry. Chapter 4 will discuss the process of finding a reputable, well-connected agent in more detail. In this business, connections are everything. An agent may have contacts with particular magazine editors, photographers, or art directors, and the agent can contact these people and suggest that they work with one of the models that he or she represents—an agent's recommendations go a long way. It is important to note, however, that an agent is not the person who chooses models for assignments. He or she can only submit your composite sheet—or comp card—to a potential client. A comp card is basically a model's business card. It tells who the model is, states his or her vital statistics (such as height, weight, measurements, etc.), indicates how the model photographs, and includes the agency's name and logo, address, and phone number so that the client may contact the agency.

Taking Care of Business

An agent is also in charge of the more tedious aspects of bookings. He or she will keep track of your appointments and bookings and will schedule your time accordingly. An agent will also get all the details of a booking for you and will communicate them to you so that there is no stone left unturned and no surprises when you arrive.

And then, of course, there's the money issue. It is your agent's job to negotiate your fee for every job you get. The agency will also take care of billing clients and will collect your fee for the job you've done. Remember, though, that it is also important for a model to develop a good business sense when it comes to financial matters. By understanding exactly what you're entitled to and by keeping close tabs on what you've earned, you can avoid any potential problems later on down the line. A reputable agent will not try to cheat you out of what you're rightfully owed, but it's better to be safe than sorry. A discussion of agency scams and what to look out for will be discussed in chapters four and five.

Making the Initial Contact

Doing research and finding a good agent to represent you will likely prove to be the difference between a mediocre career and a career in which the sky's the limit. The first step in finding an agency to represent you is to research agencies in your area. To start, you can look in the phone book and can make a list of agencies near you. Many famous models started out this way—modeling in and around their hometowns before moving on to bigger markets. You should also make a list of agencies to contact in major cities like New York City, Chicago, Los Angeles, Miami, and Toronto.

This process can be made a bit simpler by buying a directory of agents that are located in the area that interests you. You can find this kind of directory by contacting a company that specializes in modeling products and information, such as The Model's Mart. This company sells agent lists and can be contacted by calling (800) 223-1254.

The First Step

Working first from your list of local agencies, call them and ask whether or not they have "open calls" for new talent. Many agencies hold open calls every week—this is a hopeful, would-be model's opportunity to be seen by an agent and get the ball rolling. During an open call, agents meet with aspiring models and conduct a short interview. Most agencies have physical standards that a model must meet in order to be seen. For instance, a female model who is shorter than five feet, nine inches might not get an opportunity for an interview during an open call.

If you do meet these requirements and go to an open call, be sure to bring some snapshots with you that have your name, phone number, birth date, and measurements printed neatly on the back. Be sure to include clothing and shoe sizes.

If you are told that you don't meet an agency's physical requirements, send a few snapshots instead. Whether you're bringing your snapshots along with you or you're mailing them, make sure that the snapshots consist of at least one good head shot and one full-length shot. If you're sending the snapshots, be sure to include a brief cover letter in which you list your date of birth, your height, your pertinent clothing sizes, and your hair and eye color. Be sure to include your phone number and a self-addressed stamped envelope that the agent can use to reply to your letter and to return your snapshots.

Save Your Money

It is important to note that when you are initially contacting an agency, you DO NOT need to have so-called professional photographs taken to use as your snapshots. Once you have signed with an agency, your agent will assist you in putting together a good portfolio. At this stage of the game, it is unwise to spend a lot of money—potentially thousands of dollars—on a slew of expensive photographs that may or may not further your career. More often than not, the quality of these photographs will not be up to par as far as a reputable agency is concerned.

From an agency's vantage point, it is preferred that you don't have a bulging portfolio of substandard photographs. When just starting out, a prospective model is far more attractive to an agent if he or she is a fresh face who hasn't had a lot of less-than-quality exposure. If an agent is interested, he or she will usually set up a photo test for you free of charge.

Dominik's Debacle

Dominik had been told so many times that he should model that he finally decided to give it a try. It seemed logical to him to put together a portfolio first so that he would have something to take to the agencies. He looked in the phone book for a few photographers' names, made a few calls to check on the photographers' experience and rates, and went with the most reasonable price.

Dominik's photo shoot went fairly well, as far as he was concerned. The photographer seemed to know what she was doing. There were nice black-and-white photos lining the walls of the studio, and the photographer assured him that she knew just the kind of photographs he would need to sign with an agency. Dominik had figured on having about five or six photographs in his initial portfolio, just to give agencies a glimpse of what he was all about. After the first few minutes in the studio, the photographer had talked him into getting the "deluxe" package, which would allow him to "pick and choose" from a greater variety of photographs so he could "tailor his portfolio to different agencies' needs."

This sounded reasonable enough. Dominik decided that the photographer probably knew best, and he left it up to her to decide what kind of photographs she would take. When all was said and done, Dominik had a bill for $1,150 and a mediocre assortment of photographs. He began contacting agencies, all of which told him that they just needed a few snapshots, and not necessarily professional ones. Many of the agencies also told him that if he were signed, the "professional" photographs he had paid for wouldn't be used in his portfolio.

Dominik had made a mistake that many aspiring models make every day. He had rushed into putting together a portfolio and had trusted a "professional" who supposedly had his best interests in mind. Dominik could have saved himself a lot of money and time by researching what the agencies required of him.

Aiming High

Because New York City is the industry's hot spot, many aspiring models choose to start at the top and contact the city's leading modeling agencies, such as Ford, Elite, and Wilhelmina. There's nothing wrong with this approach, but know that the competition at these agencies is extremely tough, and many models already have fairly thick portfolios and lots of experience from the work that they've done in smaller markets before they contact the New York agencies. You will find the names and addresses of the major New York agencies included in the For More Information section at the back of this book.

If you live in an area that has a branch of Elite, Next, Ford, or Metropolitan close by, it is a good idea to visit all of them. These are the industry's top agencies, and they'll be able to give you a good sense of your potential. If you don't live near any of these agencies, that's okay, too. Find out which agencies in your area have the best reputation (more about this in chapter 4) and pay them all a visit or send a letter and some snapshots.

Looking and Acting the Part

Whether we're talking about a face-to-face meeting with an agent at an open call or dropping your snapshots in the mail, you have to be aware of what an agent is looking for. Of course, different agencies specialize in different kinds of models, but when it comes to first impressions, it is best to follow some basic, industrywide rules.

The Skinny on Snapshots

We've already established that every aspiring model needs snapshots, and that you should send or bring along at least two shots—a head shot and a full-length body shot. These shots should be clear and sharp and should feature you looking natural and relaxed. The head shot should be fairly close-up. Women should wear minimal or no makeup (the latter is preferred). The full-length shot should ideally be a bathing suit shot so that agents can get an idea of your proportions at a glance. It is best to have your snapshots taken in natural lighting. Have a brother, sister, or a friend (with a steady hand!) photograph you outside, either in the morning or before sunset, to avoid any harsh glare or unflattering shadows cast by a too-bright sun.

On the Ball for the Open Call

If you are going to an open call, you should look natural. Women should wear minimal or no makeup (again, no makeup is preferred). Your hair should be styled simply and pushed back off your face if possible. Men should be clean-cut. It is also a good idea to wear simple, tasteful clothing that is form-fitting enough to allow an agent to see your build easily, although your clothes should not be so tight that they look in any way binding or uncomfortable. Wear something in which you will feel confident—open calls can be a little intimidating the first time around, and you'll want to appear as poised as possible.

Selling Yourself

When you meet with an agent, the most important thing is to sell yourself and be yourself simultaneously. Tell the agent why you want to model. State briefly that you are serious about committing yourself to success. The agent should get the sense that you are friendly, take direction well, and have a strong work ethic. An agent will probably ask you an open-ended question such as "What were your expectations in meeting with me today?" Make sure that you are prepared to answer such a question. Have a definite idea what you want out of the meeting and express it clearly. If an agent feels that a prospective model is wasting his or her time with unconvincing answers—or worse, no answers at all—that model will be discounted.

It is also vital that you ask some well-thought-out questions of the agent and keep careful notes about what you learn. After all, you and the agent are both interviewing each other. Asking questions will show that you've done your homework and that you are serious about modeling. For instance:

- Ask how much money you'll have to spend up front.

- Ask how much you'll have to spend over the long term.

- Ask how long it typically takes to get work, and whether the agent feels you'll get work quickly.

- Ask about the agent's commission rate, and if that rate would ever change for any reason.

- Ask how and when you would get paid.

- Ask about the agency's hourly rates.

- Ask if the agency would require you to make any kind of changes in your appearance (such as a change in hairstyle, weight loss, or any kind of cosmetic surgery).

- Ask how the agency would market you.

Show the agent what a stellar personality you have. Agents appreciate models who can deal with clients in a professional yet energetic way. The ability to communicate is key, since agents don't want to spend their time teaching you how to interact with people. Being outgoing is a definite plus. Sure, you'll feel nervous at this initial meeting—that's to be expected—but have faith in your ability to have an intelligent conversation with the agent. Don't view this opportunity as the only one you'll ever have. If you don't contact agency after agency after agency, you're not working hard enough.

Remember, even though some agencies seem all-powerful, you are shopping for an agency that will suit your needs. It's up to you which agencies you'll contact and which ones you won't. Do your research and treat open calls as opportunities to learn about the profession. Listen closely to what each agent has to say so that you can apply it to your next open call. You might find agents intimidating because they may seem to hold the key to the future of your modeling career. However, they don't—you do.

Try and Try Again

It is best to apply to several different agencies. As we mentioned before, different agencies have different "looks" that they are known for representing. It's not a bad idea to call the agencies you're considering in advance and ask if they could send you press kits so you can see what kind of models they represent. While your look may not appeal to one agency's principal clientele, it may very well appeal to the clientele of another agency. Your best bet is to contact those agencies first whose look you feel you most closely represent.

Of course, the more agencies you apply to, the greater your chances are of achieving success. It's important to keep in mind that this is a completely subjective situation, and it may even come down to a particular agent having a bad case of heartburn on the day he or she meets with you. You cannot—CAN-NOT—take rejection personally, no matter how impossible that may seem. If you are truly determined, these rejections (and there are bound to be some) should not discourage you. If an agency turns you down and gives you some constructive criticism, implement the agency's suggestions the next time you contact another agent.

It's also a good idea to try to reapply to agencies approximately every six months. There could be many reasons an agency might turn you away the first, second, or even third time around. Maybe they already have a model signed whom you resemble. An agency will always honor the model already under contract in order to eliminate the possibility of internal competition. Maybe they are aiming for a niche for which they don't feel you're suited. Whatever the reason, remember that change is inevitable. An agency's roster of models can change from month to month, and there may be a need for your look next week, next month, or next year. You won't know unless you keep trying.

Some of the most famous models in the world were turned away from open calls because an agent didn't think they had the look the agency needed. If those models had given up, they would have missed out on fantastic careers. Take supermodel Christy Turlington, for instance, one of the most famous models in the world. She was actually signed with the prestigious Ford agency, then was promptly dismissed based on some less-than-spectacular first shots. She didn't give up, and she has laughed all the way to the bank.

Lauren Hutton, who rose to modeling fame in the 1970s, was told time after time that she needed to have the gap between her teeth fixed. She refused and ultimately she became known throughout the industry for her charming, gap-toothed smile. She continues to model today.

And of course there is Cindy Crawford, who was often told that she needed to have her mole removed when she first started out. She, too, refused, and the mole has become her trademark.

The Agency
Response

4

This is the moment you've been dreaming about.

When the Agency Wants You

Maybe you're one of the lucky ones who is able to make a connection with an agent at an open call. If this is the case, the agent will probably ask that you work with the agency for a "trial period," which is basically just the time they need to figure out whether or not your look will work well for them. During this trial period, you will be introduced to photographers who will give you test photo sessions. These photos will be assessed by the agency before you are formally signed on with them. If you've sent snapshots and the agency likes what they see, you'll be contacted for an interview. These interviews are usually conducted at the agency, but some agencies will send a scout to meet with you in the town or city where you live. Sometimes an agency will ask to see some more snapshots of you, in which case you should send them right along.

Before You Sign on the Dotted Line . . .

You can't believe your luck. The agent actually wants you.

It's an exciting situation, to be sure, but don't make any hasty moves, because a wrong decision can cause you a lot of unnecessary grief and aggravation later. You should never sign any agreements with an agent you don't know a lot about. This comes back to doing your research. Find out how many models are signed with the agency. An agency should have no problem supplying you with this information. Take a look at the agency's "book"—a collection of head shots of models represented by the agency. The book will give you an idea of how many models could compete with you for jobs. This is not to say that you shouldn't sign with an agent who has other models in your "category"— models who have a look similar to yours—but the more models in your category, the more competition. A modeling career is about getting jobs, and your odds of snagging an assignment are much higher if you're not competing with a lot of other models from within your own agency. Competition within the industry at large is rough enough.

Even if you like everything you see about a particular agency, it's a good idea to try to arrange for a trial period, anywhere between three and six months. If you're sufficiently pleased with your agent's work during this trial period and feel that you're being represented well, then you can sign a longer-term contract.

And never, *ever* sign a contract before you're absolutely certain that you understand everything in it. It's always a good idea to show the contract to a lawyer before you put pen to paper.

Decisions, Decisions

What if more than one agency wants to represent you? The decision could be a tough one to make. First, ask yourself a few questions about the agencies that are interested in representing you.

- Am I impressed with the agency's level of professionalism? Do the employees handle models and clients in an honest, straightforward way? Usually the only way to know this is to visit the agency in person and observe.

- Does the agency show enthusiasm about my modeling potential and the future of our partnership?

- How does the agency stack up to the competition? Are they well respected in the industry? You may want to call local advertising agencies and the like that use modeling agencies on a regular basis, and ask their opinions on the best agencies they've worked with and the less-than-stellar ones they have suffered through.

- How successful are the other models the agency represents? (This is usually a good gauge of an agency's success in the industry.)

- Let's not forget one of the most important questions of all: Do you like the people who work there? The importance of this cannot be stressed enough—you will be dealing with these people a lot if you sign with the agency. You need to feel comfortable with the agency's employees and be able to trust them.

Other Signs to Look Out For

If you find that you are still having a hard time making a decision, it's time to get really nitpicky. After all, it's your career on the line here. When you visit an agency, there are a few things to look for that can give you a better idea about how they do business.

- Does the agency's office prominently display photos from bookings they've gotten for their models? This is always a plus.

- Is the office busy and bustling? An office with a lot of ringing phones and busy employees usually means that the agency has a lot of business to attend to, which is a good thing.

- Take a look at the agency's models' head shots. Are they professional?

- It's not a bad idea to ask to see the comp cards of some of the models that are featured on the agency's walls. Some shadier agencies sometimes display ads that feature models who are not even signed with the agency.

An agency with nothing to hide will have no problem giving you the models' names so that you can contact them yourself.

• Listen closely to what's going on around you. Are there a lot of bookings being set up for the agency's models? If not, you may want to ask one of the agency's signed models how many bookings and go-sees he or she gets in an average week or month.

• It's always wise to ask to see the agency's book. A book features photographs of the agency's models. If you see familiar faces, this means that some of the agency's models have been booked on successful jobs that have gotten good exposure—otherwise you wouldn't recognize them!

• When you talk to the agency's models, ask how they feel about the agency. A signed model has the benefit of experience. He or she can tell you about the agency's business practices, whether the agency does its part to find its models good jobs, whether or not the agency is trustworthy in paying models for their work, and whether or not models are paid in a timely manner.

• Ask about specific clients who have hired models from the agency, then call these clients to ensure that the agency's claims are true.

The Law of Numbers

Although every situation is unique, it is a good idea to try to follow this simple rule: Never sign with the first agency you go to unless you have carefully explored other options first. This can be a hard adage to follow. Most hopeful yet unsigned models are excited about the prospect of making this first connection with an agency, and the natural tendency is to want to jump at the opportunity. Restrain yourself and go to as many agencies as you can.

Many people in the industry suggest that you visit no fewer than five agencies before you make any decision. Shoot for a minimum of five, but don't stop there if more opportunities present themselves. The modeling industry's law of numbers more often than not proves to be true—the more you see, the more you know, and the better your odds of picking the right agency.

One Last Thing

It would be great if you could trust everyone in the modeling industry, but the sad truth is that you can't. Although most agents are straight shooters and would never misrepresent themselves, there are some who will, and you need to be aware that they could do it at your expense. A model who is well aware of the possibility of agency scams will be far less likely to become the victim of one. Before you sign with an agency, be sure to check with the Better Business Bureau in that state to find out if there have been any reports of bad business dealings. If an agency has complaints stacked up against it, it is probably best to walk away.

You can find some listings for Better Business Bureau offices throughout the United States and Canada in the For More Information section at the back of this book.

It's actually a good idea to be wary of an agency even if it has only a handful of complaints against it. Chances are good that there are several unfiled complaints for every one that makes it on record. You can *never* be too careful. Protect yourself at all costs.

Portrait of a Scam

5

It's a dog-eat-dog world out there, and you might run into some wolves in sheep's clothing during your quest for an agency to represent you. You can handle it, but it helps to be aware of some of the warning signs so that you can see a scam coming from a mile away. This knowledge can save you a lot of time and money, not to mention a lot of heartache and disappointment.

Nicole's Near Miss

Nicole was at the mall, looking for a gift for her mother's birthday. As she wandered around in a jewelry store, a well-dressed man approached her.

"Pardon me, miss. I don't mean to bother you, but I work for a modeling agency in the city. Have you ever modeled?"

Nicole was a little shocked by the question. She had often thought about trying to get into modeling. Her mother had mentioned it once,

and her drama teacher at school had suggested it a few months before.

"I've never done any modeling, but I've
thought about it," she replied. "Why do you ask?"

"You have a definite look," the man said,
handing Nicole his business card. "I think
you could really do well with our agency.
Why don't you think about it and give me
a call?"

Nicole took the card and thanked him. It
was all so exciting. She tried to picture herself
shimmying down a catwalk and having her
face splashed across the covers of all the
fashion magazines. When she got home, she
told her parents what had happened.

Her mother and father looked skeptical.

"Well, I'd like to know a little bit about this
agency's credentials before you do anything,"
her mother said. "I think we should make a
few phone calls."

The next day, Nicole and her mother
called the Better Business Bureau. They were
given a laundry list of all the complaints
filed against the "agency" by young women
who'd been approached in much the same
way. It seemed that this so-called agency had
approached many attractive young women
with the same modeling pitch and then had
convinced the girls to make a deposit to
cover the costs of getting a portfolio together
and attending modeling school, both of
which were lies. There was no portfolio, and
there was no modeling school—but there

were a lot of young women who had sunk a lot of money into the so-called agency and had seen no results.

Nicole was disappointed, but her parents assured her that they could find her a legitimate agency if she wanted to pursue a modeling career. They would just need to do a bit of homework.

Of course, some legitimate agency scouts do sometimes discover new models in supermarkets, shopping malls, and even train stations, but most models have to do the legwork, visiting one agency after another before finally making that connection. The trick is to be patient and work hard.

Warning Signs

Bogus agencies and modeling scouts have all kinds of different approaches, but it helps to be alerted to some of the most obvious indications that someone is trying to swindle you. Let's say that an agency you've either visited or have sent snapshots to calls you in for a meeting. You're excited—this could mean the contract and modeling jobs you've been dreaming about. You find yourself sitting in a big room with many other hopeful candidates, and an "agent" starts rattling off a speech about how you can all be stars if you pay the agency money up front for photo shoots and modeling lessons. The cost to you is only $1,000, the agent says.

It would be safe to say that this "agency" has no clients, and doesn't need them to bring in revenue. They make money off the fees they charge you to be in their program. Get up and walk out. Better yet, run! This is a scam. Reputable agencies do not conduct business this way—ever. Any agency that is worth your time will train you free of charge and will not require any money from you until you start making money from modeling jobs booked for you by the agency. Then—and only then—should you invest any kind of money in a composite (which features several different shots on the same sheet), a head sheet, and a spot in the agency book. A legitimate agency may charge you to have your picture appear in its book. This book is what is sent to clients who are looking to hire models. In this case, be careful to cover only your part of the cost to print the picture. You should also request a copy of an agency's book so you can look it over before any money leaves your hands.

Understanding the Double-Talk

It also helps to study a page from the scam phrase book. Listen carefully to what an agent or scout says to you.

- "The deposit is fully refundable." If this were true, the agency wouldn't have you pay it in the first place. What this really means is that your deposit may be refunded only in the event that you meet some very specific conditions—and just about no one meets these conditions. The legal loopholes are well thought out, and that's how the money is made.

- "Our program is very selective. We have experts who will assess your talent and who choose only the best models to participate in our program." Not exactly. They will take whomever wants to be in the program and will give them the money they ask for.

- "Don't worry about the money. We guarantee it will be refunded to you in full if you're not selected to participate in our program." There will be no refund. They take anyone who will pay the money they ask.

- "If you don't have the money up front, we can work something out. After you get some assignments, we'll just deduct the money from your pay." They get paid regardless of whether they find you jobs or not. That will likely be in very small print on the document they want you to sign.

- "You are guaranteed that you'll be working immediately." No agency can guarantee that, and no good agency would make such a sweeping claim.

- "We're a major player in the modeling world." This could very well be true, if you're talking about Elite, Ford, or Metropolitan, for instance. But you can pretty much figure that this kind of claim in a smaller city or town is nonsense and that the agency is misrepresenting itself.

- "There happens to be just one opening in our modeling class. You can take it now, but if you don't, we'll have to give it to someone else." There is always "just one opening." A good agency wouldn't pressure you this way, and typically wouldn't make you take a class, either. Your training should be free of charge if an agency is really interested.

- "Our photographer is the best in the country. You'll have to get your pictures done by him if you want to sign with us." This is one of the biggest scams in the business. It deserves its own section.

The Photographer Scam

You should absolutely question an agency that tells you—after assuring you that you'll be the next big star—that in order for the agency to sign you, you have to use a specific photographer designated by the agency for your head shots, composite sheets (comp cards), etc. Remember that a reputable agency brings in money by getting jobs for the models it represents—the agency takes a percentage of the models' payments per job, usually somewhere between 10 and 20 percent. An agency that demands that models use a specific photographer is very likely up to some shady dealings.

A reputable agency may suggest that you work with a certain photographer that has a great reputation within the industry, but warning lights should start flashing if an agency insists that you have only one choice. The scam scenario usually goes something like this: The agency sends would-be models to a photographer who actually works for the agency. The models pay this photographer a fee (which is usually exorbitant), and the photographer kicks the money back to the agency.

An agency that is working this kind of photographer scam will usually put a pretty convincing spin on it to lure a hopeful model into committing his or her money to this photographer. The agent might tell the person that he or she is just a bit off the mark at the moment—but with the perfect photos, the agency could start sending him or her on big jobs, maybe even in New York. These are empty promises meant to wear down the person. The agent might then pull a contract from a drawer, awaiting a signature so that the appointment can be set up to take some pictures.

Of course, you should never sign anything unless you know what it contains. In a case like this, you could expect to see within that contract a tidy sum of money listed as the price for the photo session, perhaps $1,000 or more. By signing that contract on the spot, you've committed yourself to paying that money to the agent for what would likely be a less-than-quality photo session with a "photographer" who is in cahoots with the agency. It is more than likely that the agent would never let that contract leave the room, even if the model-in-the-making requested to take it home in order to read it more carefully. The agent might respond to such a request by saying that trust is key in a model's relationship with an agent, and that the model can show his or her trust by signing the document right there on the spot. If this happens, get up and leave.

The Modeling-School Scam

Some agencies will insist that you go to a modeling school in order to sign with them. This works in much the same way as the photographer scam. You pay money to take classes at the modeling school—which is affiliated with the agency—and the agency makes money off the fee that you pay. Do your research to make sure that a modeling school is legitimate. You can pretty safely assume that if a school is affiliated with a specific agency, the school is less than reputable.

Not Every School Is a Scam

It is important to note that there are many legitimate schools. These schools teach the correct posture, how to move properly in front of the camera, how to care for your skin and hair, how to apply makeup, how to communicate effectively, and how to develop your portfolio. They will usually also teach proper nutrition and exercise techniques. Some schools may give acting lessons—a skill that can be helpful for television commercial models.

Attending such schools can improve a prospective model's confidence, which is a plus no matter what your vocation. Keep in mind, however, that attending a modeling school should never be a prerequisite for signing with an agency or becoming a model. It is not a necessary step, it is merely a helpful one if you feel you could use a little boost to get you ready for a modeling career. Some agents like to see that someone has attended a reputable modeling school—after all, an agent's bottom line is money, and a well-trained model who already knows some of the ins and outs of the business is likely to bring in money more quickly.

Some reputable modeling schools may help you make connections with good agencies by having agency representatives come in to take a look at their graduating class. Every once in a while, a particular student whom an agent or scout feels shows a lot of promise may be chosen to go to New York, for instance, and meet with a well-established agency. Realize, though, that a model who shows that much promise could achieve the same results by sending a few photos through the mail, or even by taking part in a modeling contest put on by a well-respected agency. These routes cost the hopeful model far less money.

Contests and Internet Agencies

Many reputable agencies hold contests each year. If a model wins one of these contests or places as a finalist, his or her career can kick into high gear. Prominent agencies then take these models under their wings and help them develop the skills they need to succeed in the industry. A winning model could become an agency's new face. If this happens, the possibilities are endless.

But be sure to do your research. Not all contests you read about in the backs of fashion magazines are legitimate. Many charge a high entrance fee, then put together a flimsy contest that likely has no bearing on the winner's career. Some well-known and respected contests can be found listed in the back of this book.

It's also wise to be wary of Internet-only agencies and "schools" that conduct business solely via the Internet without the benefit of person-to-person contact. If an agency or school conducts money transactions and handles all contractual affairs over the Internet, it's best to avoid them altogether. Currently there are no strict laws in place to protect you from potential Internet scams.

The Bottom Line

You need to know that being accepted into a modeling school does not mean that you are guaranteed a career as a model. A modeling school cannot give you modeling potential if you don't have it to begin with. A reputable modeling school can only enhance the potential you already have. The hard, cold fact of the matter is that many (if not most) modeling schools will allow almost anyone to attend if that person has money to spend, and there is absolutely no promise that the person's money will be earned back with modeling jobs. If you feel that you'd like to attend modeling school to polish up your appearance, be sure first and foremost that the school is not affiliated with a questionable agency. You will also want to keep a few other helpful hints in mind if you plan on enrolling in a modeling school (these apply to agencies as well).

- Be wary of schools that use high-pressure tactics to get you signed up. A modeling school should never require that you sign a contract or document on the spot.

- If the school doesn't accept any form of payment other than cash or a money order, walk away. This is a pretty definite signal that they only want your money and could care less about your future. Good schools usually don't charge a registration fee up front, either.

- The school should be more than willing to give you references—names, addresses, and phone numbers—for models who have gone through their program and have gotten good jobs as a result of what they have learned.

- Find out if the school is licensed (which is required by many of the states in the United States). You can check this with the state attorney general. The school's license should be current and in good standing. For schools in Canada, you can check with the Better Business Bureau for this kind of information.

- Check to see if there are any outstanding complaints filed against the school by contacting the state attorney general or your local Better Business Bureau.

- If you think that you'd like to enroll in a modeling school, you should visit several before you make your choice. Study the roster of classes each school offers, then compare the curricula so that you can decide what best suits your needs. You may even want to ask if you can attend a class free of charge in order to get a feel for how the school does things. Find out who teaches the classes and look into the teachers' credentials and qualifications.

- Take a careful look around each place you visit and take notes for yourself. Is it a busy place? Are the phones ringing? Typically, the busier, the better. Also, most schools have photos of models on the walls. Are these models graduates of the school? There's no harm in asking. Check out the models' hair, clothing, and makeup. Do these photos look current, or have they been hanging up there for years?

- Take a look at the other people the school is enrolling. Do they seem to have the potential needed to be models? If they do not, walk away.

- Don't hesitate to ask specific questions regarding the school's policies. Do they work with any international agencies? If so, which ones? Do these agencies send their people to the school to scout out new talent? If so, how often? Have any of their graduates been signed with those agencies? If so, have they gotten a lot of work?

• Be wary of any school that tells you that it will completely take care of your portfolio in a one-shoot deal. Good portfolios take a bit of time to put together. An upstanding school will know this.

• If the school does recommend a specific photographer, ask to look at that photographer's portfolio. If he or she is good, about three-quarters of the portfolio should consist of tear sheets from magazines.

• Last, but certainly not least, trust your instincts. If it feels wrong, it probably is.

It's always smart to bring someone with you—either a parent or another adult you trust. This will help make you feel more comfortable and may nip any of the school's questionable tactics in the bud. If you do your research and decide to enroll in a modeling school, make sure you have everything in writing. A promise that has been spoken but not written holds no legal water, which means you have no legal recourse should you feel you've been wronged. Maintain good records and keep them in a safe place.

Chantal Scopes It Out

Chantal was ready to try her hand at modeling. She had contacted an agency in her area and had sent them a few snapshots of herself. The agency told her it would be a good idea for her to enroll in a modeling school so she could be well prepared for the business. They even recommended a particular school. Chantal had read up a bit on how to get into modeling and wasn't entirely convinced that school was a necessary step, but she contacted them anyway.

A week later, Chantal went to her appointment at the school. She listened as the admissions coordinator told her all the wonderful things that would happen to her after she graduated. He guaranteed Chantal that her career would skyrocket and that she'd make a lot of money because she'd be heads and shoulders above the competition. All she needed to do was pay $2,500 in cash for the twelve-week course, and for a small extra fee the school would take care of her portfolio, too.

Chantal asked all of her questions. Was work guaranteed in writing? How many potential models attended the school? What were the instructors' credentials? Did the school work with only one photographer? What had previous graduates of the school gone on to accomplish? Could she please have a list of graduates to contact?

Chantal noted that the man didn't look too comfortable. He sidestepped many of the questions and threw in the fact that there were only a few slots left in the classes. These, he assured her, would go fast, so it would be best if she signed up quickly to avoid losing out on the opportunity.

Chantal thanked him and said she would think about it. As she walked out, she knew exactly what she thought about it. It was a scam.

Let the Modeling Begin

6

Maybe you've gone to a modeling school; maybe you haven't. Maybe you've sent snapshots to several agencies; maybe you've gone to visit the agencies in person. After all your research, fact-checking, and patience, your hard work has paid off. You've been signed by an agent that you trust, and you're beginning to get jobs. Now the next phase begins.

The Portfolio

Once you start getting booked for jobs, it is time to start thinking about your portfolio. A portfolio is a model's most important tool. Quite simply, you use your portfolio to sell yourself as a model. A portfolio should be composed of your best photographs—photos that show your versatility and unique qualities. Very often, people who are in a position to hire you won't even see you in person. They will see your book. Actually, they will usually contact several agencies and will likely see hundreds of books from hundreds of models before they decide whom they want to see in person so that they can seal the deal. This is why your portfolio has to sell itself—you will not be there to sway their decision.

Some models do put together a portfolio before they sign with an agency—they have a professional photographer (or photographers) work with them. It's a matter of personal preference. It's not necessary, and it can become quite an expense. Many agents would prefer to build your portfolio with you. Most important, a good portfolio takes a bit of time to put together.

A common mistake many beginning models make is to throw their books together in a mad rush, thinking that the faster they do this, the faster their careers will get rolling. This is not the case. Because a good portfolio is vital in getting good jobs—and thus good exposure, so you can get great jobs—patience and great care are required in putting together the right selection of photographs. Your portfolio should showcase your strengths in such a way that a client can get a handle on what you'd be able to sell, whether it's clothes, lipstick, or hiking boots. A good agent will have a good sense of which photographs work and which don't, and he or she will painstakingly help you build a strong portfolio that will make a client pick you out of the crowd. Sometimes you may have a different idea than your agent has about what photographs to include, but realize that an agent is more familiar with the clients' needs than you are.

At this point, you should have a definite idea of what your strengths are—perhaps you have a phenomenal body, or great skin and hair, or beautiful hands. Concentrate on your outstanding traits and have a photographer get some great photos that will show potential clients why they should choose you.

Meeting the Photographer

A trustworthy agent won't insist that you use a specific photographer, but he or she will probably suggest a couple of photographers and arrange for you to see them so that you can take a look at their portfolios. Some of these photographers may have styles that appeal to you more than others. You can arrange to work with the photographers you feel best suit you. It's a good idea to work with more than one photographer—this allows for a true variety of shots to showcase different looks.

It is best to ask your agent's advice about which photographers would best be able to capture your look in the most marketable way. If, for instance, your look is more appropriate for *Seventeen* magazine than it is for *Cosmopolitan,* your agent will suggest photographers who are known for shooting in the *Seventeen* style, not photographers who will shoot you in a low-cut, sequined dress and dramatic makeup, a la *Cosmopolitan.* If you have the makings of a catalog model, your agent will hook you up with photographers who are experienced in catalog shoots. Once you have a few really strong photographs, your portfolio is well on its way. Over time, as you are booked on different jobs, your portfolio will begin to grow.

As a rule of thumb, your initial portfolio should include the following:

- A minimum of two head shots, ideally featuring two different moods. For instance, one shot should show your smile, the other should show a more introspective expression, or there could be an outdoor shot and a studio shot.

• A full-length body shot that shows your proportions. These are often taken of the model in a bathing suit or in underwear. It's best to go with what you're most comfortable with and to make sure it shows your entire body—from head to toe—in the most flattering way possible.

• A minimum of two fashion shots, featuring you wearing casual clothes and wearing something more formal. It's fairly standard for men to include a shot of themselves in a suit and tie, and for women to include a shot of themselves in a skirt, dress, or pantsuit.

• If you have a special, active skill—such as skiing, rock climbing, or mountain biking—it's not a bad idea to include a shot that shows you involved in that activity to give your portfolio a sense of variety. Remember, you are selling yourself. You have to work with photographers to present yourself as a multi-faceted model.

Your special talents can give you the edge you need to snag a job. Over time, as you are booked for different jobs, your portfolio will begin to grow and change. It will get better and better as you are booked for more jobs—you can add your newer tear sheets and remove those that are less current or that no longer represent the image you intend to portray.

Your agency will be able to assist you in choosing the best shots for your book. You may come across a situation in which you feel very strongly that a certain shot should be included, while your agency may advise against it in favor of a different shot. It is usually best to trust your agency in such matters, since they have the benefit of experience.

The Comp Card

Once you have had some work assignments that have produced good shots—and you and your agent have assembled your initial portfolio—it's time to prepare a comp card, or composite. A composite serves as a model's business card and is vital in marketing you to potential clients. A beginning model's comp card could be a reproduction of a great test shot that states the model's name, agency, and vital stats. It may consist of one photograph from a portfolio, or it may feature several photos on the front and back. Some agencies use laser copies of portfolio photographs. A model and his or her agent work at putting together the most professional, eye-catching composite possible.

Many models mistakenly believe that the more photos included in the composite, the more jobs he or she will book. This is entirely false. Quality, not quantity, is the key. Your composite should feature only your very best photographs. Starting out, you will not be expected to have a very fancy, expensive comp card—however, your comp card should be professional and should show you at your best, even if the design is simple and it includes just a photograph or two. As you develop in your career, so will your composite.

Starting out, your composite will probably measure eight inches by five and a half inches, and it will most likely be printed in black and white or as a color photocopy. Black and white is cheapest when it comes to printing costs, and you'll want to keep expenses down at this point until you have been successfully booked for several jobs. Again, patience is the name of the game. Give yourself a chance to develop your modeling skills and personal style before you invest in a color composite, since this is an expense that you, not your agent, will be expected to cover. If the photos are exceptional, it does not matter if they are black-and-white or color prints. When you do invest in a color composite, be sure that the photos included will stand the test of time—if you think that the photos may be outdated in six months because they show the trend of the moment or a very trendy clothing style, do not include them. You will have invested your hard-earned money for nothing.

When you and your agent select photos for your comp card, you will have to consider the type of work for which you are aiming. A model who will be pursuing editorial work will want his or her photographs to portray a different look than a model who is pursuing catalog work. For instance, an editorial shot might be very stylistic, featuring the model in a dramatic pose, outfit, or setting, whereas a catalog shot would be much more straightforward, simply portraying the model in a particular outfit. The photographs should communicate the type of work for which your agent feels you are best suited.

On average, you will have to have several hundred to 1,000 comp cards printed the first time around, and these will go to clients who currently use the agency's services or have done so in the past. You should also have a supply of comp cards on hand at all times in your portfolio. Every time a model goes to a casting call or on a go-see, he or she will be expected to give the client a composite to keep. Yes, the client has likely already seen the model's portfolio, but the composite is a way of leaving a calling card to ensure that the client remembers you. This first composite should last for about the first year, but it may have to be redone sooner should the model's look change during that time.

The Book and the Head Sheet

Like the composite, the agency book and head shots are also important marketing tools. All agencies have some kind of compilation of materials that they use to promote their models. The larger, more established agencies have books, the pages of which are models' comp cards. An agency's book consists of composites of each and every model the agency represents, and it is one of the agency's primary ways of promoting itself. Because so much of the agency's business relies on its book, it is important that the book be as professional looking as possible. The book must be glossy and eye-catching, and it must be put together with only the highest-quality materials.

This, of course, costs money to produce. A model should expect to pay anywhere from a few hundred dollars to upwards of $1,500 to have his or her composite included in the agency's book. The bigger and more prestigious the agency, the higher the price to be featured in the book. The price will also depend on how much space on a book's page you request. The fee is usually deducted from the model's pay for future assignments, but it is money well spent. An agency's book will be circulated among photographers, clients, and other agencies both nationally and worldwide, so a model could be booked for an international assignment based on the exposure his or her agency's book provides.

The model is in charge of getting his or her comp card in to the agency by the agency's specified deadline. Late submissions can delay the book's production unnecessarily, which affects the entire agency. On average, an agency puts out its book about once every eighteen months.

Many agencies also put out a poster featuring small head shots along with the names of their models. This is called a head sheet. The head sheet is another great promotional tactic—it is given to potential clients and photographers who can hang it on their walls for quick reference. When a photographer or client has a specific look in mind, the agency's head sheet is at his or her fingertips.

The Model Image

7

Perhaps more than any other career you could have, modeling focuses on your appearance. Yes, genetics have a lot to do with what a model looks like—there are stories of models eating nothing but fried chicken and sausage gravy and still maintaining a rail-thin physique, or models with lightning-speed metabolisms and naturally long, thin limbs. Many models claim "good genes" as their saving grace.

For those prospective models who have never had to watch what they eat or make time for exercise, it's important to know that good genes can't cover their bases forever. That should get a cheer from those whose genes don't allow such indulgences. A successful model must maintain a good complexion, a well-toned body, a regimen of proper exercise and nutrition, and an adequate sleep schedule to ensure that he or she projects the most attractive image possible all the time. This can be quite time-consuming, but it is essential considering the fact that a model who is polished and healthy will get more jobs than will the model who eats nothing but hamburgers and chocolate shakes. The biggest investment you can make in your modeling career is taking care of yourself.

A Healthy Lifestyle

The way you care for your body is reflected in the image you present to the world—and modeling is all about image. Poor health habits can make your skin look bad, your hair look lifeless, and your body feel tired. This can dull your edge over your competition. Of course, you should take care of yourself regardless of whether or not you are a model, but modeling places extra pressure on you to positively sparkle all the time. This constant sparkle doesn't usually come naturally—most models have to work at it and make time for healthy choices.

Modeling is generally a pretty fast-paced lifestyle, and some models succumb to the vices that run rampant in the modeling industry. There are photos in magazines of well-known models smoking. Many models insist that smoking helps them control their weight. The truth is that smoking turns your teeth yellow, is bad for your skin, and can ultimately kill you. That's not so pretty. There are also stories of models who do drugs to keep them going because their schedules are so hectic. These models often get hooked on drugs and ruin their careers—not to mention the fact that they put their lives at risk. Being responsible for your own body means that you have to make smart choices and steer clear of any substance or behavior that can hurt you.

Skin That Glows

Healthy skin is a model's best friend. If you care for your skin properly so that it is smooth and glowing, the camera will capture this. Many young models think that they don't have to practice any kind of skin care routine until their skin starts to show signs of aging. Don't put off until tomorrow what you can begin today. Beginning a disciplined skin care regimen will ward off premature aging.

It's recommended that a model make an appointment with a facialist to learn more about his or her skin type. Once you know what kind of skin you have—be it oily, dry, combination, or sensitive—you can then devise a skin care routine and choose skin care products that suit your skin type. Facials should be a religious part of your skin-care program, since a facial can deep clean your pores and exfoliate your skin properly. You can also maintain healthy skin by using the following tips.

- Cleanse your face and neck each morning and evening using products that compliment your skin type.

- Eat a well-balanced diet that includes a variety of foods.

- Drink at least eight 8-ounce glasses of water each day—more if you can. This keeps your body hydrated and your skin fresh.

- Be sure to wear sunscreen at all times, even in the winter, to prevent sun damage, and stay out of the sun whenever possible.

- Do not squeeze pimples, as this can cause excessive irritation.

Your Hair

Your hair is one of your most visible assets, so you need to treat it with care. Find a good stylist and colorist (if need be) with whom you feel comfortable. You can ask your agency for recommendations. Be sure that the style and color you choose suit your face and the image that you are trying to convey. Models must contend with styling products, and their hair is constantly being blow-dried, curled, straightened, and crimped. All of this can dry out hair, so you must take precautions. Here are some general hair care tips.

- Get a trim approximately every six to eight weeks to get rid of split ends and prevent breakage. If your hair is colored, you should maintain this same schedule for color maintenance.

- Don't ever cut or color your hair on your own. Leave it to the professionals. Often, photographers and stylists will have very specific ideas about what style and color your hair should be for a particular shot.

- Handle your hair with care. Wet hair is particularly susceptible to breakage and should be combed gently, never brushed.

- Condition your hair often, and try to have a conditioning treatment at a salon once a month.

- Remember that for work purposes, you may need to sport a particular hairstyle that you're not so fond of. It's one of the drawbacks of the job, but keep in mind that a hairstyle you don't like can get you jobs you wouldn't get otherwise. And besides, hair always grows back!

You Are What You Eat

Your diet is an important part of how you look and feel. Your diet affects your skin, your hair, your nails, your body, and your energy, so it is imperative that you eat well. A balanced diet will give you the proteins, carbohydrates, vitamins, minerals, and fats—yes, fats—that your body needs for peak performance. Most models are expected to maintain thin bodies, but this does not mean that they can't eat, which is an unfortunate and often damaging myth that leads many models down the road to eating disorders and severe health problems.

The secret is to eat healthy foods—such as lean meats, low-fat dairy products, fruits, vegetables, and whole-grain pastas and breads—and to avoid foods with excessive sugar, fat, or bleached flour. A healthy diet combined with a regular exercise program will keep you strong and fit while helping you maintain a slim and trim physique.

As a model, you will be on the go all the time. If you don't eat properly, you will not have the energy to keep up with your busy schedule. It can be difficult to find the time to eat properly with so many demands on your time, but it is imperative if you want to realize your maximum potential as a model.

Eating-Disorder Dangers

Because the modeling industry is full of fierce competition, many models become obsessed with their weight and develop dangerous eating disorders in their attempts to stay thin. Some implement unhealthy fad diets. Some develop anorexia and starve themselves until they are nothing more than skin and bones. Some develop bulimia, going on food binges and then vomiting. Some abuse laxatives to get rid of food as fast as they take it in. They do all of these things so they can be "thin enough."

The pressure to be thin can be overwhelming for models, who may hear from agents and even photographers that they aren't "thin enough." Sometimes models will be promised all kinds of jobs if only they'd "lose a few pounds." It can be difficult to maintain a healthy body image and a healthy diet with such negative reinforcement. Yes, most straight-size models have to watch their weight diligently to avoid having pounds creep up on them—that's one of the drawbacks of the job—but it's important to remember that your health is the most important thing. If a model who is five foot nine and weighs 125 pounds is told she needs to lose weight, she is being lied to, plain and simple. One person's opinion should not sway your eating habits.

Not only do disorders such as anorexia and bulimia wreak havoc on your looks—always a concern for a model—they can damage your body beyond repair and can even kill you. Nothing is worth that. Being aware of the warning signs can help you spot any potential problems before they spiral out of control. If you notice that you are relying on fad diets, diet pills, laxatives, or diuretics to control your weight, this is cause for concern. If you go for long periods without eating, obsess over calorie counts and fat grams, or develop a tendency toward bingeing and purging, you may be developing an obsessive relationship with food that could lead to anorexia or bulimia.

Depression and compulsive exercising are also red flags to look out for. If you develop any of these behaviors or feel that you have any hint of an unhealthy attitude toward food, you should immediately talk to someone about it—be it a doctor, a psychologist, or your agent. These people will know how to help you find the balance you need to cope with the pressures of modeling and to stay healthy at the same time.

Just Say No

Too much partying is another danger many models face. The modeling industry is known for its fast pace and, unfortunately, for its often reckless habits. It can be easy to fall in with a partying crowd that drinks too much and that does drugs. Some models make the harmful and often fatal mistake of adopting these habits to fit in and to be accepted.

This is a choice that is yours alone to make. No one can force you to drink too much or to take drugs, and your career will not suffer if you refuse to party. In fact, just the opposite will be the case. A model who has his or her head on straight, who arrives on time and is sober for appointments, and who looks healthy and rested will get more jobs than will the model who arrives late to appointments looking like something the cat dragged in, or who misses appointments altogether. In the fashion industry, time is money. Clients, photographers, makeup artists, art directors, hairstylists, agents, and so on will not tolerate an out-of-control model wasting their time. Partying too much is a sure-fire way to get a bad reputation and lose jobs, and your agency may fire you for it. Not to mention that it can destroy your looks, ruin your health, and even kill you. The choice seems clear, doesn't it?

If you develop a problem with drugs and/or alcohol, don't be afraid to talk about it with someone who can help you get the help you need. You may choose to talk to a parent, a sibling, a friend, a doctor, or a counselor. You may even want to talk to your agent, who will have experienced similar situations before. He or she should know how to handle yours. Admitting that you have a problem is nothing to be ashamed of. It takes a lot of courage, and people will respect your honesty and your efforts to deal with your problems. If a model refuses to admit that he or she has a problem with drugs and/or alcohol, and the substance abuse affects the model's job performance (which it is eventually bound to do), an agency may very likely drop the model from its roster. Often, the agency's contract with a model includes a substance abuse clause, giving the agency the legal backing it needs to terminate contractual obligations should such a situation occur. If a model has signed such a contract and is found in breach of the substance abuse clause, he or she will have little or no legal recourse to fight the termination.

A Model's Day

8

By this point, it's clear that modeling requires a lot of hard work. What makes modeling different from most other jobs is that a model never knows from one day to the next what his or her schedule will be like. Many people find this kind of hectic lifestyle appealing, but this can be difficult for people who prefer a set daily routine. This is something to take into account—the modeling lifestyle can become draining fairly quickly, especially if you don't know what to expect.

Preparing Yourself

Organization is key to a model's success. Because a modeling career is less structured than is a typical nine-to-five job, a model sometimes must work hard to avoid feeling overwhelmed by daily schedules that are often haphazard at best. A daily planner is a must for a model—it can help you keep track of all the people you must see, the places you must go, and the times you must do these things. This can all become a jumbled mess if you don't have a clear way of keeping track of this information. You can also use your planner to keep track of expenses you've incurred so that your agency can reimburse you if necessary. Such records are also useful to keep for tax purposes.

A cellular phone is a great idea, since you'll have to check in with your agency frequently to find out about any go-sees, bookings, or auditions that have been set up for you. With a cell phone, your agency can contact you while you are on the go. An answering machine is essential. If your agency can't contact you via cell phone, it can leave a message on your machine, which you should check every few hours to learn of new developments in your schedule.

The Schedule

A model's day begins before the alarm clock ever goes off. He or she must actually begin preparing the day before, checking in with the agency around five o'clock each weekday to be updated about the next day's commitments. At this time, the agent gives the model the list of appointments that have been set up for the following day. Most of these appointments will be scheduled for weekdays during normal work hours. These appointments should be recorded faithfully in a planner, accompanied by all pertinent names and addresses. As a model just starting out, you will spend a lot of time running from client to client and meeting with photographers to show your portfolio, allowing them to also see you in person.

A model must usually be up early in the morning—around 7 AM—to prepare for the day. Punctuality is very important, because clients and photographers will not tolerate lateness. If the model has a booking that day, he or she should allow a bit of extra time in case of travel delays and the like. A studio booking can last anywhere from an hour to an entire day, depending on the nature of the booking. An agent will schedule the model's other appointments accordingly. A go-see—where a model "goes and sees" a client for a prospective job—can last anywhere from a few minutes to several hours, depending on how interested the client is in the model. Go-sees will be discussed in greater detail a bit later in this chapter.

A Trip to the Studio

A model must also know how to conduct himself or herself at a studio booking with a client or photographer. Keep in mind that the job is the most important thing. Professionalism is paramount, even if the studio atmosphere is extremely laid back. Photographers and clients also love a well-prepared model. If you have been asked to bring a specific wardrobe, be sure to have it on hand, and be sure that it is clean and wrinkle-free. You should also bring along a bag containing the items you may need for the shoot—your "model's bag." This bag should be with you everywhere you go. You can adjust the bag to suit a particular booking once you've learned what you need to bring along. Although different assignments within different markets require different items, here's a quick rundown of what you should have on hand to throw into your model's bag should the need arise. As always, it's best to be prepared for anything.

For Women:

- Bras, underwear, and slips in white, beige, and black

- Pantyhose in neutral colors, white, off-white, and black

- A few pairs of shoes (heels and flats in off-white, black, and brown; white sneakers)

- A few well-chosen, simple accessories (jewelry, belts, scarves, etc.) that will go with many different outfits

- A one-piece swimsuit

- Hygiene products (deodorant, manicure kit, tampons, razor, toothbrush, toothpaste, etc.)

- Hair care items (some good brushes and helpful styling products)

- Makeup (skin care products, sponges, foundation and concealer, powder, a few shades of blush, a few eyeliners in different shades, eye shadow in light, medium and dark neutral shades, eyelash curler, mascara, two shades of lipstick and lip liner, nail polish in a neutral shade)

- A sewing kit

- Your portfolio and comp cards

For Men:

- White underwear briefs (these are usually preferred to boxers)

- Socks in several colors (including white, gray, black, and brown)

- A few pairs of shoes (dress shoes and casual shoes in black and brown, white sneakers, and sandals)

- Shirts (dress shirts and casual/sports shirts in a few different colors)

- Pants (dress pants and casual pants)

- Jeans

- A turtleneck and sweater

- Swimsuits (trunks and briefs in solid colors)

- Hygiene products (deodorant, shaving kit, nail kit, toothbrush and toothpaste, etc.)

- Hair products (brush and comb, styling aids)

- Foundation and powder that match your skin tone

- A sewing kit

- Your portfolio and comp cards

Yes, these are lengthy lists (especially for women), but you can put your bag together gradually, as you are booked for more and more jobs. Often, a client or photographer will have most of what you need on hand, and will request you bring just a few items.

A Few Closing Pointers

- When you go to the studio, make sure that you are prompt, and that you introduce yourself to everyone present to establish a friendly rapport. It's a great idea to write down the names of everyone you meet with a note about what their role is in the studio, be it client, photographer, art director, assistant, hairstylist, or makeup artist.

- Because time is money in the modeling industry, efficiency is important. Listen carefully to any comments and/or directions a client, photographer, or art director gives you so they will not have to take the time to go over it twice.

- If you need anything that you did not bring with you, be sure to ask permission to do so.

• When it comes to modeling clothes, be careful not to get any kind of food, drink, or makeup on yourself. Once you are done modeling a particular outfit, take it off immediately and hang it up so it doesn't wrinkle. A client will appreciate your efforts.

• You may want to ask if you should be wearing dress shields to protect any garments you may be modeling from perspiration stains.

• Above all else, the two most important things you can bring to a booking are professionalism and a willingness to embrace the client's or photographer's ideas. Making a good impression means good word of mouth within the industry, and more jobs for you.

The Go-See

As discussed earlier, the go-see is when a model goes and sees a client in order to be considered for a particular job. During a go-see, the client can check out a model in person rather than simply looking at an agency book or head sheet. A go-see is like an interview or audition—it is an opportunity to convince a potential client that you have what it takes to do the job.

A model's day may be peppered with go-sees with different clients, and these go-sees might come about in different ways. Sometimes the agency might arrange for a model to have a meeting with a potential client even if there is no particular job at the moment. This is a general meeting so that the client can be made aware of a model's capabilities and possibly can choose the model for a job when it becomes available. Sometimes clients will contact an agency if they have an hour or two free to arrange to meet with the agency's "new talent," or they might ask for a go-see with a model who has the certain look they are searching for. If a client has received a model's comp card from an agency and has expressed interest, a go-see will be set up. Clients are always looking for the perfect models to market their products and will scour different business and social functions within the industry. If clients spot models that interest them, the client will request a go-see.

A go-see can be a little intimidating for a model just starting out, but that is to be expected. The more go-sees you have, the more comfortable you will become with the process. First, be sure that you are dressed appropriately if the client has specified a certain look. If no dress code has been specified, ask your agent what he or she feels would work best. It is also important always to be prompt and to introduce yourself to the receptionist as soon as you get there. As a general rule, there will usually be several other models who have been asked to meet with the client, so it is likely that you will have to wait to be seen. Delays are common, so expect them. If the delay interferes with other appointments you have that day, you can politely tell the receptionist, who may be able to get you in more quickly.

When you are taken in to see the client, introduce yourself one more time and specify who your agent is. A firm handshake is also a good idea. Sit down only if you are invited to do so—many clients conduct interviews with the model standing to get a better idea of the model's physical attributes. You should always have your portfolio with you so the client can look it over.

Once you meet the client, you have to sell yourself. The client is usually looking for a specific "type" to market the product—which is why you've been called in the first place—so all the models at the go-see will probably share similar traits. You must convince the client that you are the one for job. The client may ask what you can offer that the other models can't. Be prepared for questions of this nature, and have well-thought-out answers ready. The trick is to appear calm and self-assured (even if you don't feel that way!) so that the client will also have confidence in your abilities. Be friendly but professional, and let your personality shine through.

Meetings with clients can be over quickly or can last awhile, depending on the situation. Typically, you can tell that the meeting is over when the client gives your portfolio back to you. At this point, leave your comp card with the client and thank him or her for meeting with you. If a client tells you to keep your comp card, don't worry—you may not be right for the current assignment. If you handle yourself professionally, you could very well be in the running for upcoming jobs.

A Model's Money

To be a successful model, you must have a good grasp of the financial aspects of the business. This comes down to being organized and responsible. If you don't have a clue what's happening with your money or how you should handle tax issues, investments, and the like, you could be setting yourself up for a financial catastrophe. Unlike the typical nine-to-five job, modeling is an entity unto itself, and you need to know all the ins and outs of money management in order to protect yourself.

The Model-Agency Relationship

As a model, your agency's job is to promote you and find you work. Models don't make a set annual salary. You are paid by the job. Basically, you employ the agency to help you make money, and the agency takes some of that money for its efforts. A model's commission to an agent varies depending on his or her contract, but the average rate is between 10 and 20 percent. That means that if a particular job paid $1,000, the agent would make between $100 and $200. Looking at the larger picture, if a model made $50,000 in a year, his or her agent's take would be between $5,000 and $10,000. That may seem fairly steep, but an agency employs many people and must incur many expenses to ensure that its models make connections with clients. The commission fee is the price a model must pay for the agency's expertise and networking capabilities.

You are also paying for the agency's billing of clients and collection of the fees clients pay you for the work you do. After the agency has billed the client and the client has paid the fee, the agency will then issue you a check for the job with the agency's commission already deducted. You may also see deductions taken for any expenses you are responsible for that the agency has covered—such as putting out a head sheet and having a photo included in the agency book for promotional purposes. Generally, though, the agency will usually only deduct its commission and any cash advances they've given you. The agency will not deduct taxes from your checks because you are not an employee.

Self-Employment

When you work with a modeling agency, you are considered self-employed. As an independent contractor, you are in charge of recording everything that pertains to your earnings and any expenses incurred while performing your job. You must cover your own social security taxes as well as your health and disability insurance, and you are responsible for figuring out your income taxes and making sure they are paid. This is a lot to keep track of, so it is absolutely necessary that you keep impeccable records.

You will have to pay your federal and state taxes four times a year, once at the end of every quarter. If you live in the United States, the important dates to keep in mind are April 15, June 15, September 15, and December 15. If you live in Canada, your tax payments will be due March 15, June 15, September 15, and December 15. Because your taxes must be paid by these dates, you must have enough cash on hand to cover the amount. If you fail to make your payments, you can be hit with large penalties and can end up having to pay a lot more than the original amount.

For this reason, it is a good idea to hire an accountant. He or she can help you figure out the amount you need to sock away in order to cover your quarterly tax payments. An accountant can also help you fill out and send in all of the pertinent paperwork. If you live in the United States, make sure that the accountant is a certified public accountant—C.P.A. for short. In Canada, look for a chartered accountant, or C.A. Tax laws are always changing, and a C.P.A. or a C.A. is obligated to stay current with the laws in order to keep his or her license. It is recommended that you use a C.P.A. or a C.A. who is well acquainted with the modeling industry so that special deductions or consider-ations specific to the business will be kept track of. Ask your agency to recommend an accountant.

Hiring an accountant doesn't mean that you can pass off all responsibility for your earnings and let someone else take care of the details—you should be aware of everything that is happening with your money at all times—but your accountant can help you find the most straightforward way to document your fiscal situation. If you don't keep up your end of the bargain or if you neglect to keep detailed records of your earnings and expenses, your accountant will not be able to prove any business-related deductions and you will end up paying more taxes as a result.

Money Management

When you begin working as a model, it is a good idea to open a separate checking account. Any monies you receive from modeling can be deposited into this account, and you will thus have a clear idea of exactly what your income is. Keep a detailed account of all deposits made into the account, and save all bank statements to make sure that the amounts correspond. If you live in the United States, each year your agency should send you a document called a Form 1099 that lists your earnings for that year. In Canada, the form is called a T4. Compare the form to your records to make sure that your income has been reported accurately.

Also, be diligent in keeping records of any money you've put out that relates to your career, as some of these expenses can be deducted. Your accountant will be able to tell you what can and cannot be included in your tax deductions. If you neglect to keep receipts and detailed lists of the money you've spent, the taxes you pay will be on your gross income, and the money you could have deducted from that amount will be lost in the shuffle. To make record keeping easier, try to use a business credit card or to write checks from your income checking account.

Although your accountant can go over your own personal expenditures in detail, it helps to have a general idea of goods and/or services you may be able to deduct. Agency fees and commissions count, as do accounting fees. Money spent on cosmetics, hair, nails, and clothing may also be deducted if it can be clearly documented that the expense was necessary for your job. Travel expenses such as airfare, lodging costs, car rental, and food can be deducted if they pertain to modeling jobs. If traveling out of the country, be aware of the exchange rate and note it for your records so your accountant can take that into consideration.

You should also keep track of the money you spend on composites, prints, or anything having to do with your portfolio, as well as money spent on seminars or classes associated with your career. If you incur entertainment expenses—taking an associate to lunch, for instance, with the idea that the person will be instrumental in how your career develops—you may be able to claim this as a deduction as well. These are the major deductions, but your accountant can go over your records carefully and can include appropriate deductions.

The Final Word

This may all seem a bit confusing, but once you find a good accountant and start keeping careful records of everything you earn and spend, it will get easier. A model without a financial plan can end up squandering much of the money he or she has rightfully earned, when that money could be put to work to make even more money. A successful young model needs to think about retirement plans and other worthwhile investments now, so that he or she is well taken care of down the line.

Looking Toward the Future

10

After modeling for a few years, you may be ready to move on to something else and to explore other things that life has to offer you. However, you may not be ready. One of the drawbacks to a career in modeling is that it sometimes has to end before you want it to. As mentioned earlier, the modeling industry is fueled by youth. Many people are afraid to age, afraid to be confronted with their mortality. In the modeling industry, a thirty-five-year-old model who by any other standards is still young and vital will likely not get as many jobs as will an eighteen-year-old model.

Of course, there are exceptions. Today, there are many more mature models than there were even twenty years ago. People are taking better care of themselves and are living longer, and many clients want to appeal to this older age group to sell their products. For the most part, though, modeling is a short-term career, and you need to plan in advance for what will come eventually. In chapter 1, we stressed the importance of a good education and the need to develop other skills and talents besides modeling so that you will be ready to begin the next phase of your life when modeling is no longer as lucrative.

Perhaps you have an interest that is related to modeling, such as photography, clothing design, advertising, or fashion merchandising, or maybe you'll choose to pursue something entirely different, like computer science or law. It's best to have a plan. Being prepared will give you peace of mind, and it's never too early to start exploring your options. You'll be glad you did!

Considering Commercial Acting

A popular route that many models take after their modeling career has drawn to a close is commercial acting. Commercial acting is in many ways an extension of what a model has had to do during his or her modeling career. Modeling is very much about acting, usually without words, and convincing the public through your body language and facial expression to take notice of a particular product. A successful model can further hone his or her skills in the world of commercial acting. After all, film is film, whether you're talking about still photography or moving pictures. If a person's image translates well onto film, that person could have a successful career in commercials and other kinds of film work. If you want to get into commercial acting, it is wise to consult an acting agent to represent you. You should follow the same steps in choosing an acting agent that you would for choosing a modeling agent. Many modeling agencies either have acting divisions or are well connected to agencies that specialize in acting.

Types of Commercial Acting Jobs

Models are often used in two main types of commercials. There is the "non-air commercial," which consists of audience-reaction commercials that are not broadcast, client demos, and copy testing. Usually still photographs are taken, then the pictures are converted to video. There are also commercials that involve the actor moving in front of a video camera in both speaking and nonspeaking roles. These commercials are usually broadcast. They may feature the actor eating potato chips or fast food, shopping at a certain grocery store, washing his or her hair with a certain shampoo, or applying lipstick.

Work in speaking commercials may require voice training, since clients will want a model who can both speak and act. Sometimes a model will be cast based only on his or her looks, but it's best to develop commercial speaking skills in order to increase your prospects. As a commercial actor, you would be either a principal actor (the main actor in the commercial) or an extra (a member of a crowd scene, for instance). Of course, being the principal actor carries a bit more weight and looks good on a résumé, but being an extra can offer some great opportunities. As an extra, you can get experience and can learn how a commercial is put together. You also can learn who does what on the set and can study the principal actors to see what you should be aiming for.

If you plan to go into commercial acting, you will likely have to enroll in some training classes. These classes can teach you things that might never even occur to you—how to hold a product so it can be seen easily, how to time your words as you move, or even how to drink a glass of juice in a way that will look good on film. You can also take specific classes to brush up on auditioning etiquette. Agents who deal in commercial acting recommend that an aspiring actor take a "cold-reading" class, because a given commercial's dialogue, or copy, will not always be made available to auditioning actors before the audition begins. Sometimes an actor must take the copy and deliver it on the spot on the first read-through. Improvisational acting classes are also recommended so that you can learn to feel more comfortable with acting out spontaneous situations in front of an audience.

The Audition

When you do snag an audition, you'll need to keep a few pointers in mind in order to put your best foot forward. The most important thing is conducting yourself professionally. Promptness is required—if you're not on time, the audition will definitely go on without you. Wearing neat clothing suitable for the audition is also a must. If you are auditioning for a speaking role and you have been given the copy beforehand, be sure that you know your lines so well you could recite them in your sleep. Pay close attention to what is going on around you, and listen carefully to directions. If you feel nervous, don't worry—that's totally normal. However, try to project self-confidence regardless of how jittery you may be feeling. You have to believe in yourself and believe you are the best person for the part.

Rather than bringing along a portfolio, the commercial actor must have on hand a flattering head shot (black and white)—also called a glossy—and a professional-looking résumé. A glossy should be eight inches by ten inches, and should consist of your head and the tops of your shoulders. Usually, your name is printed beneath the picture. Your pose in the photo should be direct and no-nonsense. The photograph should be taken with your face as the focal point, and your appearance (clothing, makeup, hair, facial expression) should express the image you want potential clients to come away with when they look at your glossy. It's best to keep your image simple and to steer away from anything that appears too high-fashion. Potential clients should see you as a person who could be anything, not just a particular hairstyle or a trendy outfit.

Your résumé is a one-page listing of your experience for the past two to three years. You can list your name, height and weight, your agency, your pertinent training and education, any acting credits, and your unique skills and talents. It's best to leave out your modeling experience, as many casting people may unfairly look down on models-turned-actors. Feel free to ask your agent to help you put together the most impressive résumé possible.

The Payoff

Commercial acting can be a lucrative way to earn your living. As a principal actor, you can make tens of thousands of dollars for a commercial that airs nationally. This amount includes your initial payment and the residuals that will be paid to you for as long as the commercial is aired. If you become a member of the Screen Actors Guild—SAG for short—and have made enough money within a given year, you can be eligible to receive free health benefits as well. The Screen Actors Guild is a union that protects actors within the film industry.

Work Hard, Live Well

The world of modeling may seem mysterious—its secrets known only by those on the inside—but it's all pretty straightforward once you know the tricks of the trade. Now you're armed with the information you need to put your best foot forward should you choose to pursue a career in modeling. The trick is never to stop learning and striving to be your best. If you expect modeling success to come easy to you, you will very likely be disappointed. While there are the rare fairy-tale stories of models being discovered and skyrocketing to fame and fortune, this is hardly the typical route, and even those unbelievably lucky models have to work hard and keep up their ends of the bargain once they achieve success.

Good models are not made by the industry . . . they make themselves, with a little help here and there. No matter how attractive you are, if you're not willing to work hard and put up with some rejection along the way, you can be lost in the shuffle. In that way, modeling is a job like any other.

Glossary

agency book Book put together by an agency that features a comprehensive collection of photographs of the agency's models.

anorexia Eating disorder characterized by eating very little as a means of weight control.

booker Another name for an agent.

booking Modeling job.

bulimia Eating disorder characterized by bingeing on food, then inducing vomiting as a means of weight control.

composite sheet 8 x 5 1/2-inch card that features a model's photograph (or photographs) along with his or her name, statistics, and agency information.

exfoliate To get rid of dead surface skin cells by gentle scrubbing.

glossy 8 x 10-inch black-and-white head shot that a commercial actor brings to an audition.

go-see Appointment during which a model meets—or "goes and sees"—a prospective client.

haute couture Expensive, one-of-a-kind fashions created by the world's leading designers.

head sheet Promotional poster put together by an agency featuring the names and small head shots of the models the agency represents.

head shot Close-up photograph of a model's face and sometimes the tops of the shoulders.

open call Set time during which an agency meets with and interviews hopeful models.

parts model Model who makes a living modeling a certain body part, such as hands, legs and feet, or hair.

portfolio Model's collection of photographs from bookings that he or she uses to market himself or herself.

roster Listing of models that an agency represents.

runway Platform along which models walk in a fashion show.

scout Person from a modeling agency who looks for new talent.

straight-size model Female model who is a size eight or smaller. The fashion industry relies primarily on straight-size models to sell clothes.

tear sheet Photograph taken of a model that appears in a magazine.

10/20 model Another name for a plus-size model. 10/20 models can range in size from a size ten to a size twenty.

For More Information

Modeling Agencies in the United States

New York

Click Model Management, Inc.
129 West 27th Street, 12th floor
New York, NY 10001
(212) 206-1616

Elite Model Management
111 East 22nd Street
New York, NY 10010
(212) 529-9700

Ford Models, Inc.
142 Greene Street
New York, NY 10012
(212) 219-6500
Web site: http://www.fordmodels.com

New York Model Management
596 Broadway, Suite 701
New York, NY 10012
(212) 539-1700
Web site: http://www.newyorkmodels.com

Next Model Management
23 Watts Street
New York, NY 10013
(212) 925-5100
e-mail: newyork@nextmodels.com
Web site: http://www.nextmodels.com

Q Model Management
180 Varick Street, 13th floor
New York, NY 10014
(212) 807-6777
e-mail: nyc@qmodels.com
Web site: http://qmodels.com

Wilhelmina Models, Inc.
300 Park Avenue South
New York, NY 10010
(212) 473-0700
Web site: http://www.wilhelmina.com

Chicago

Aria Model and Talent Management
1017 West Washington, Suite 2C
Chicago, IL 60617
(312) 243-9400
Web site: http://www.ariamodel.com

Arlene Wilson Model Management
430 West Erie Street, Suite 210
Chicago, IL 60610
(312) 573-0200
e-mail: chicago@arlenewilson.com
Web site: http://www.arlenewilson.com

Elite Model Management
58 West Huron Street
Chicago, IL 60610
(312) 943-3226
Web site: http://www.elitechicago.com

California

Ford Models
8826 Burton Way
Beverly Hills, CA 90211
(310) 276-8100
Web site: http://www.fordmodels.com

San Diego Model Management
438 Camino Del Rio South, Suite 116
San Diego, CA 92108
(619) 296-1018
Web site: http://www.sdmodel.com

Wilhelmina Models, Inc.
8383 Wilshire Boulevard
Beverly Hills, CA 90211
(213) 655-0909

Southeast

Arlene Wilson Model Management
887 West Marietta Street

Atlanta, GA 30318
(404) 876-8555
e-mail: atlanta@arlenewilson.com
Web site: http://www.arlenewilson.com

Click Model Management, Inc.
1688 Meridian Avenue
Miami Beach, FL 33139
(305) 674-9900

Irene Marie Model Management
728 Ocean Drive
Miami Beach, FL 33139
(305) 672-2929
Web site: http://model.de/miami/im-mia.htm

Midwest

Arlene Wilson Model Management
807 North Jefferson Street, Suite 200
Milwaukee, WI 53202
(414) 283-5600
e-mail: milwaukee@arlenewilson.com
Web site: http://www.arlenewilson.com

Go International Model Management
3351 Valley View Road, NE
Lancaster, OH 43130
(614) 554-6974
Web site: http://www.go-international.com

The I Group Model & Talent Management
29540 Southfield Road, Suite 200
Southfield, MI 48076
(248) 552-8842

e-mail: igroup@kennon.com
Web site: http://www.theigroup.com

Southwest

Donna Baldwin Talent
2150 West 29th Avenue, Suite 200
Denver, CO 80211
(303) 561-1199
e-mail: info@donnabaldwin.com
Web site: http://www.donnabaldwin.com

Mirage Talent Agency
2509 South Clermont Street
Denver, CO 80222
(303) 504-4581
e-mail: MirageTalent@aol.com
Web site: http://www.mirage-models.com

MMG Male Model Group, Inc.
4465 South Jones Boulevard, Suite 122
Las Vegas, NV 89103
(702) 868-1400

Page Parkes Models Rep
3303 Lee Parkway, Suite 205
Dallas, TX 75219
(214) 526-4434

Northwest

Seattle Models Guild
1809 Seventh Avenue
Seattle, WA 98101

(206) 622-1406
Web site: http://www.smgmodels.com

Modeling Agencies in Canada

Ontario

Elite Model Management
477 Richmond Street, West
Toronto, ON M5V 3E7
(416) 369-9995

Ford Canada
385 Adelaide Street, West
Toronto, ON M5V IS4
(416) 362-9208
Web site: http://www.fordmodels.com

Québec

Folio Montréal
295 de la Commune Ouest
Montréal, PQ H2Y 2E1
(514) 288-1037
e-mail: info@foliomontreal.com
Web site: http://www.foliomontreal.com

Alberta

Grant Models International, Suite 400
604 1st Street, SW
Calgary, AB T2P 1M7
(403) 264-9585
Web site: http://www.grantmodels.com

Select Model Management Ltd.
306 Edmonton Center
Edmonton, AB T5J 4H5
(780) 482-2828
Web site: http://www.compusmart.ab.ca/select/
agency.htm

Saskatchewan

MG Model and Talent Management
241 5th Avenue North, lower level
Saskatoon, SK S7K 2P3
(306) 653-3830

British Columbia

VMH Models
1311 Howe Street, Suite 200
Vancouver, BC V6Z 2P3
(604) 221-4080
e-mail: info@vmhmodels.com
Web site: http://www.vmhmodels.com

Model Searches and Contests in the United States

American Modeling and Talent Association
510 Haddington Lane
Peachtree City, GA 30268
(404) 487-6656

Blush Models Management
2 Pomperavg Office Park, Suite 102

Main Street South
Southbury, CT 06488
e-mail: ModelSearch@Blushmodels.com

Elite Model Look
111 East 22nd Street
New York, NY 10010
(212) 529-9700

Ford Supermodel of the World
142 Greene Street
New York, NY 10012
(212) 219-6500
Web site: http://www.fordmodels.com

International Fashion Model and Talent of the Year Contest
1 Bank Street
Stamford, CT 06901
(203) 325-3138

International Modeling and Talent Association
1432 East Northern
P.O. Box 44726
Phoenix, AZ 85064
(Held in January and July; Los Angeles and New York)

Modeling Association of America International, Inc.
250 Doyle Street
Orangeburg, SC 29115
(803) 534-9672
(held in March—New York)

Model Search America
588 Broadway, Suite 711
New York, NY 10012

Pro-Model Model Search
1828 West Lewis
Pasco, WA 99301
www.pro-model.com
(send photos)

Seventeen Magazine
850 Third Avenue, 9th floor
New York, NY 10022
(212) 407-9700

The Southcentral Model and Talent Convention
1235 Whipple Avenue, NW
Canton, OH 44708
(216) 477-4227
(held in June—Atlanta)

The Southwest Model and Talent Convention
4840 Hollow Ridge Road
Dallas, TX 75227
(214) 349-6341
(held in October)

Wilhelmina Mode Model Search
300 Park Avenue South
New York, NY 10010
(212) 473-0700
(for plus-size models)

Model Searches and Contests in Canada

The Canadian Model & Talent Convention
121 Dundas Street East, Suite 202
Belleville, ON K8N 1C3
(613) 965-1783
(held in March)

Elite Look of the Year
477 Richmond Street West, Suite 301
Toronto, ON M5V 3E7
(416) 369-9995

Faces West
1008 Homer Street, No. 212
Vancouver, BC V6B 2X1
(604) 629-3463
(held in November)

Ford Supermodel of Canada
385 Adelaide Street West
Toronto, ON M5V IS4
(416) 362-9208

Fresh Faces Model Search
Stages Model Agency
2206 Dewdney Avenue, Suite 304
Regina, SK S4R 1H3
(306) 757-8370
(held in October)

Modelling Association of Canada
176 Rupert Street
Thunder Bay, ON P7B 3X1
(807) 345-2126
(held in February)

"You've Got the Look"Annual Model Search
NBY Productions
2479 Howard Avenue
Windsor, ON N8X 3V7
(519) 977-6832
(held in May)

Better Business Bureau Listings in the United States

California

The Better Business Bureau
3727 West 6th Street, Suite 607
Los Angeles, CA 90020
(900) 505-1000
email: info@losangeles.bbb.org
Web site: http://www.bbb.org

The Better Business Bureau of San Diego
5050 Murphy Canyon, Suite 110
San Diego, CA 92123
(858) 496-2131
email: info@sandiego.bbb.org
Web site: http://www.sandiego.bbb.org

Sacramento Valley BBB
400 S. Street
Sacramento, CA 95814
(916) 443-6843
email: info@sacramento.bbb.org
Web site: http://www.sacramento.bbb.org

Illinois

The Better Business Bureau Chicago and Northern Illinois
330 North Wabash, Suite 2006
Chicago, IL 60611
(312) 832-0500
email: info@chicago.bbb.org
Web site: http://www.chicago.bbb.org

New York

Better Business Bureau
741 Delaware Avenue, Suite 100
Buffalo, NY 14209
(716) 881-5222
Web site: http://www.upstateny.bbb.org

The Better Business Bureau of Metropolitan New York
257 Park Avenue, South
New York, NY 10010
(212) 533-6200
email: bbb@bway.net
Web site: http://www.newyork.bbb.org

Long Island Better Business Bureau
266 Main Street
Farmingdale, NY 11735
(212) 533-6200

Texas

The Better Business Bureau of Metropolitan Dallas
1600 Pacific, Suite 2800
Dallas, TX 75201
(214) 220-2000
Web site: http://www.dallas.bbb.org

The Better Business Bureau of Metropolitan Houston
5225 Katy Freeway, Suite 500
Houston, TX 77007
(713) 868-9500
email: bbbinfo@bbbhou.org
Web site: http://www.bbbhou.org

Better Business Bureau Listings in Canada

The Better Business Bureau of Metropolitan Toronto
7777 Keele Street, Suite 210
Concord, ON L4K 1Y7
(905) 761-0015
Web site: http://www.toronto.bbb.org

The Better Business Bureau of Montréal
2055 Peel Street, Suite 460
Montréal, PQ H3A 1V4
(514) 286-9281
Web site: http://www.montreal.bbb.org

The Better Business Bureau of South Central Ontario
100 King Street, East
Hamilton, ON L8N 1A8

(905) 526-1112
Web site: http://www.hamilton.bbb.org

The Canadian Council of Better Business Bureaus
Heritage Place, Ninth floor
155 Queen Street
Ottawa, ON K1P 6L1
(613) 751-4443
Web site: http://www.canadiancouncilbbb.ca

Modeling Web Sites

http://www.fordmodels.com
The official Web site of the Ford Modeling Agency

http://www.howtomodel.com
This site offers tips on commercial modeling.

http://www.modelnews.com
This site offers tips to the beginning model, and features
a helpful section on industry scams.

http://www.models.com
This site offers modeling news and agency profiles.

http://www.modelsinternational.com
This site offers information and professional advice to
beginning models.
http://www.newfaces.com
The Insiders Guide to Supermodels and Modeling

http://www.supermodel.com
This site offers information on the Model Search

America contest, as well as information and advice about the modeling industry.

http://www.themodelregistry.com
This site is an online virtual modeling agency that promotes models, agencies, photographers, and actors and offers pertinent industry news.

http://www.wilhelmina.com
The official Web site of Wilhelmina Models, Inc

For Further Reading

Boyd, Marie Anderson. *Model: The Complete Guide for Men & Women*. New York: Peter Glenn Publications, 1997.

Debbie Press Staff. *Your Modeling Career: You Don't Have to Be a Superstar to Succeed*. New York: Allworth Press, 2000.

Esch, Natasha, and Christine Walker. *The Wilhelmina Guide to Modeling*. New York: Simon & Schuster Trade Publications, 1996.

Feher, Patri. *The Business of Professional Modeling: A No-Nonsense Manual to Help You Create "a Marketable You."* Fairfield, CT: Spinach Publications, 1995.

Gearheart, Susan W. *Opportunities in Modeling Careers*. Lincolnwood, IL: VGM Career Horizons, 1999.

Maiwald, Sue. *Exposed!: How to Become a Model Without Getting Scammed*. Highlands Ranch, CO: Mailwald Productions, 1998.

Marcus, Aaron R. *How to Become a Successful Commercial Model: The Complete Commercial Modeling Handbook.* Baltimore, MD: Marcus Institute of Commercial Modeling, 1997.

Matheson, Eve. *Modeling Handbook.* New York: Henry Holt, 1989.

Morris, Sandra. *Beauty Manual.* Lincolnwood, IL: Lowell House, 1999.

Morris, Sandra. *Catwalk: Inside the World of the Supermodels.* New York: Universe Publishing, 1996.

Morris, Sandra. *The Model Manual: Everything You Need to Know about Modelling.* Buckingham, UK: Orion Publishing Group, 1998.

Peter Glenn Staff. *International Directory of Model & Talent Agencies & Schools.* New York: Peter Glenn Publications, 1999.

Peter Glenn Staff. *New York City Model Agency Directory.* New York: Peter Glenn Publications, 1998.

Preston, Karl. *Modelmania: The Working Model's Manual.* Marina Del Rey, CA: Dog Gone Books, 1998.

Quick, Harriet. *Catwalking: A History of the Fashion Model.* Edison, NJ: Book Sales, Inc., 1999.

Ragnarsson, Huggy. *Elite Street: The Elite Model Look: A Fashion & Style Manual.* New York: Universe Publishing, 2000.

Rejaunier, Jeanne. *Runway to Success: How to Become a Model.* Raleigh, NC: C & M Online Media Incorporated, 1997.

Rose, Yvonne. *Is Modeling For You?: The Handbook and Guide for the Young Aspiring Black Model.* Los Angeles, CA: Amber Books, 1997.

Rubinstein, Donna, and Jennifer K. Bloom. *The Modeling Life.* New York: Berkley Publishing Group, 1998.

Scesney, Stuart J. *How to Enter the Business of Commercial Modeling: A Simple Guide for New Talent & Resource Directory for the Pros!* Cockeysville, MD: The Talent Factory, 1999.

Schuller, Catherine. *The Ultimate Plus-Size Modeling Guide.* New York: Emerging Visions Enterprises, 1996.

Sommers, Annie Leah. *Everything You Need to Know About Looking and Feeling Your Best: A Guide for Girls.* New York: The Rosen Publishing Group, Inc., 2000.

Sommers, Michael. *Everything You Need to Know About Looking and Feeling Your Best: A Guide for Guys.* New York: The Rosen Publishing Group, Inc., 2000.

Summers, Barbara: *Skin Deep: Inside the World of Black Fashion Models.* New York: Amistad Press, Inc., 1998.

Tobey, Cheryl L. *The World of Work: Choosing a Career as a Model.* New York: The Rosen Publishing Group, Inc., 2001.

Williams, Roshumba. *The Complete Idiot's Guide to Being a Model.* New York: Alpha Books, 1999.

Index

About the Author

Kerri O'Donnell received her degree in journalism from New York University. She is a writer and editor currently living in Buffalo, New York.

Series Design

Daniellle Goldblatt

Layout

Thomas Forget